EVERY MAN A WARRIOR

HELPING MEN SUCCEED IN LIFE

Book 3

MONEY, SEX, WORK, HARD TIMES, MAKING YOUR LIFE COUNT

BY LONNIE BERGER

NAVPRESS

Discipleship Inside Out®

Discipleship Inside Out®

NavPress is the publishing ministry of The Navigators, an international Christian organization and leader in personal spiritual development. NavPress is committed to helping people grow spiritually and enjoy lives of meaning and hope through personal and group resources that are biblically rooted, culturally relevant, and highly practical.

For a free catalog go to www.NavPress.com
or call 1.800.366.7788 in the United States or 1.800.839.4769 in Canada.

EVERY MAN A WARRIOR is a ministry of The Navigators.

The Navigators are an interdenominational, nonprofit Christian organization, dedicated to discipling people **to know Christ and to make Him known.** *The Navigators have spiritually invested in people for over seventy-five years, coming alongside them one-on-one or in small groups to study the Bible, develop a deeper prayer life, and memorize the Scripture. Our ultimate goal is to equip men and women to fulfill the Great Commission of Matthew 28:19 to* **"Go and make disciples of all nations."** *Today, tens of thousands of people worldwide are coming to know and grow in Jesus Christ through the various ministries of The Navigators. Internationally, over 4,000 Navigator staff of 64 nationalities are serving in more than 100 countries.*

Learn more about The Navigators at www.navigators.org.

You may download and reproduce any of the resources from the website EveryManAWarrior.com. These have been provided by the author for your benefit.

EVERY MAN
A WARRIOR
Helping Men Succeed in Life

EVERY MAN A WARRIOR is a discipleship course designed to help men succeed in life. It is for men who want to become the warriors God intends, not living lives of mediocrity, but maturing and becoming equipped in the areas where men fight and need to win.

These areas include:
- Walking with God
- Marriage
- Raising Children
- Managing Money
- Going through Hard Times
- Work
- Sex and Moral Purity
- Making Your Life Count

Overview of the *Every Man a Warrior* Series

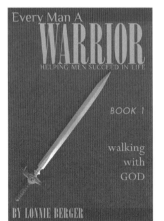

EVERY MAN A WARRIOR is a discipleship Bible study series for men comprised of three books. Here is how the course is put together:

Book 1 Walking with God

The first nine lessons of EVERY MAN A WARRIOR develop the essential skills of discipleship. These skills are: Having a Quiet Time, Meditating on Scripture, Prayer, and Application of the Word. These skills are then applied to the topics in the next two books. It is important that all men go through Book 1 before starting Books 2 and 3. Book 1 includes the EVERY MAN A WARRIOR verse pack and all course verses.

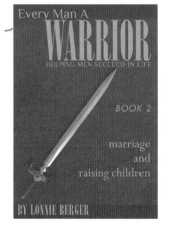

Book 2 Marriage and Raising Children

These eight lessons give practical help and a biblical outlook on both Marriage and Raising Children. It comes with a special emphasis on raising teenagers. These lessons have profoundly impacted the lives of men wanting to become better husbands and fathers.

Book 3 Money, Sex, Work, Hard Times, Making Your Life Count

Book 3 has ten lessons that bring scriptural application to the issues of Money, Sex and Moral Purity, Work, Going through Hard Times, and How to Make Your Life Count. After family, these are the issues that most consume a man's life and where he needs to succeed.

Single men may choose to use only Books 1 and 3.

How to Use This Study

Book 3 of the *EVERY MAN A WARRIOR* series is designed for men who want help in their personal life. These areas include: managing money, going through hard times, sex and moral purity, work, and making your life count for something eternal. If you have not completed Book 1, it is important that you do so. Much of the content in Book 3 will be missed if you have not learned the skills taught in Book 1.

In a Small Group

Using *EVERY MAN A WARRIOR* in a small group of four to six men is optimum. These groups normally meet in the evening. Some groups have met successfully early on Saturday mornings or during the week before work. A time slot of ninety minutes is needed for groups. *Some of the lessons are long and may require two weeks to adequately discuss the material.*

One-on-One

This study can also be used to disciple men one-on-one, such as over lunch, and can be accomplished in sixty minutes.

A Men's Sunday School Class

Book 3 can be used in a Sunday school class. However, because of the length of the lessons, most will take two weeks to complete depending on the time allotted for your class. That's okay. Because of the importance of these topics, we do not want to rush through the material. In fact, these lessons may be some of the most important Bible studies you will ever do.

Groups that meet in a Sunday school class will need to pair off and share Quiet Times and review verses in groups of two in order to save time. Then the whole group comes back together to read the stories and discuss the lesson.

Always start the second week on the lesson by reviewing verses and sharing Quiet Times. These disciplines are the core of your walk with God and are the most effective tools we have to bring about transformation. The longer you are in an accountability group, the deeper these spiritual disciplines will take root in your life.

Write Your Own Points to Remember

In Book 3, starting with lesson 6, we will learn a new skill. Each of you will write your own *Points to Remember.* This exercise will help you review the lesson and grasp more deeply the key thoughts that need to take root. Use a highlighter or underline key parts to facilitate writing your own *Points to Remember.*

Note to Leaders

Be sure to read The Leader's Guide on page 11, before your first meeting.

The web page ***www.EveryManAWarrior.com*** includes a downloadable pdf file with some thoughts on how to effectively lead a group. It is titled, **How to Start and Lead a Group.** As the leader, read these pages before your first meeting.

You can download the weekly Leader's Guide from the Web page to make it easier to follow while leading the lesson. It is important to follow the Leader's Guide even if you have led other Bible studies. It comes from two years of field testing and is designed to help your group succeed. Some men find the disciplines of Quiet Times and Scripture memory especially hard and want to skip those parts of the course. Following the Leader's Guide will insure that these items will not be left out ***and makes the Leader's Guide the course disciplinarian, not you!*** Using the Leader's guide gives you the greatest potential to have a successful study.

CONTENTS

BOOK 3

MONEY

GOING THROUGH HARD TIMES

OTHER ISSUES FOR MEN

APPENDIX

FOREWORD

Men,

For the last 30 years I have watched God shape and prepare my good friend, Lonnie Berger, for this unique ministry contribution. *Every Man a Warrior* reflects God's work in his life and in the many lives of men God has allowed him to disciple, counsel, and be involved with in their personal spiritual transformation.

Men deal with issues every day that test their core values, integrity, and spiritual manhood. Issues like financial management, suffering, sex, moral purity, work, and making one's life count is the stuff that shapes a man's character. *Every Man a Warrior* hits these gut issues head on with no sugar coating.

As you progress through the course, each lesson of *Every Man a Warrior* will be a life changing experience. I guarantee that you will sense God transforming your values, and character and bringing you to a new level of spiritual maturity.

But don't stop with yourself. As you experience God reshaping your life, share *Every Man a Warrior* with a small group or another individual. It will be an investment that transforms the men you disciple and impacts future generations.

Hang on, here we go!

Lauren Libby, President and CEO of Trans World Radio International

INTRODUCTION

Congratulations! You have finished Book 1, the discipleship section of *EVERY MAN A WARRIOR.* Now you possess skills to have an effective Quiet Time, memorize verses, pray, and meditate on the Scripture. *These skills needed to be built into your life before addressing the areas where we as men fight and need to win.*

Gentlemen, you are going to learn how to fight. In the next ten weeks, you are going to get trained and equipped to:

- Fight to keep money and material possessions in the right perspective, being personally prepared to provide for your family and future, yet free to be involved in that which will last for eternity.
- Fight to walk with God and be a man who does what's right even when suffering and situations are tough.
- Fight to make your life count for something eternal.
- Fight to stay morally pure.
- Fight to view your job and career from God's perspective.

We will make these topics our focal point for Quiet Times, Scripture memory, meditation, and Bible study. We will explore foundational biblical passages and target practical application. If you do the work, you will come out of this course a better man—more highly skilled to win the battles you face in life.

Book 3 will deal with some potentially sensitive areas of your life. *Remember, any personal information shared in this group is confidential and not to be shared with anyone, even your spouse.*

FOR THOSE WHO FINISH BOOK 2

The *EVERY MAN A WARRIOR* Series was designed so that single men could skip Book 2 and go directly to Book 3. You will need to assign a leader to each of these lessons, taking turns leading the study just as in Book 2.

Leader's Guide to

LESSON 1
MONEY AND CONTENTMENT

NOTE TO NEW LEADERS

You can download the Leader's Guide from the website *www.EveryManAWarrior.com* to make it easier to follow while leading the lesson. It is important to follow the Leader's Guide while leading the lesson. While some items are the same each week, others are special, one-time instructions that will negatively impact the study if missed. These items are marked with a star. ★

MONEY AND CONTENTMENT

✓ Break into pairs and recite all your previously learned verses to each other.

✓ Open the session with prayer.

✓ Go around the room, asking each man to share one Quiet Time.

★✓ Page 9: Read the Introduction to Book 3.

✓ Begin reading the lesson paragraph by paragraph.

✓ Pages 12–18: Read and discuss each Bible verse. Ask each of the questions on these pages. Depending on time, have two to four people give their answer. Try to include everyone.

✓ Page 17: Read the *Points to Remember* and discuss the following question.

✓ Pages 17–18: Read and discuss *Possible Applications*, the *Financial Principle*, and the *Assignment.*

★✓ Page 18: Point out that they should have their Quiet Times on the suggested Scripture passages.

✓ Page 18: Place Mark 4:19 in the front window of your *EMAW Verse Pack* and memorize it this week.

✓ End the session using the *WAR* method of prayer.

Money and Contentment

Jack and Karen thought they had it made. Jack had just landed his first job with a prestigious law firm. They were on their way!

Jack and Karen had been sweethearts since grade school. Growing up in a rural area of Kansas, Jack was the high school football hero and Karen was the prettiest cheerleader. They never had eyes for anyone else and married in college.

After they married, Jack needed to finish his law degree, so Karen dropped out of college to help put him through school. Jack knew he would land a good job some day, so he had no problem borrowing money to keep them from scrimping too much. They lived the good life and hoped for the future.

Working for a prestigious law firm turned out to be much harder than Jack had first thought. The long hours and pressure to produce billable hours for the firm was much tougher than expected. Jack had a generous starting salary of $60,000 per year. He never stopped glowing when he saw how proud his dad was of his accomplishments.

Jack's dad used to brag about his son's income, the things they could buy, and the house they had purchased. Jack agreed with his dad: they had arrived—and they should have the nicest things money could buy.

During the first five years, Jack's salary increased. But so did their outflow. They bought a new four-bedroom home in a prestigious neighborhood and filled it with expensive furniture. Karen kept expressing concern that they were spending a lot of money, but Jack brushed it off. They could afford it! Since Karen was working full-time as a receptionist, they ate out a lot and took long vacations. There seemed no limit to what they could afford with the sixteen credit cards they had, and they had no problem making the minimum payment each month. When they started having children, Karen stopped working outside the home, which reduced their income. But Jack was not worried. Things were great!

Ten years after college, life began to crumble. Jack and Karen had three children ages seven, five, and two. The glamour of his high-intensity job had worn off. Each month they were still paying on college loans, a new SUV, and another four-year-old vehicle. The sixteen credit cards had now grown to twenty-seven; some were charged to the limit. Jack's earnings had leveled off, but he continued to spend freely. Some months they could not pay the minimum required on all their credit cards.

Then it hit. Karen had a strange illness. The medical professionals could not figure out what was wrong. She had constant fainting spells, spent weeks in the hospital for tests, and at one point almost died. Jack missed a lot of work and the medical bills began to pile up. His insurance did not always cover all of Karen's medical expenses, something he had not anticipated. She eventually recovered, but by then they found themselves in financial shambles. To pay the bills, Jack took out a large second mortgage on their house, leaving them owing more than the house was worth. A $1,600-per-month first mortgage, the $600 second mortgage, and two car payments totaling $800 were consuming a big portion of Jack's pay.

But the worst part was the credit card debt. It now totaled $85,000—and many of the creditors wanted to be paid in full. Just the minimum balances for the twenty-seven cards ran more than $1,800 per month. Creditors frequently pestered them at home trying to get payments. Karen, still recovering, was so upset that she feared answering the phone. Threatening letters from bill collectors began to stack up.

In the midst of this, the older vehicle, just recently paid off, needed $1,200 of repairs. Without telling Karen, Jack decided to trade for a one-year-old Camry costing $30 a month more than what they had been paying. When he drove it home Karen went ballistic! *"How could you?"* she exploded at Jack. But with communication strained, Jack would not talk about it or curb his spending habits.

As Karen reflected on their situation, she began to see that whenever Jack felt stress, he bought something. His closet at the time boasted twenty-four suits, thirty-eight sweaters, fourteen pairs of shoes (some costing $300) with boxes of things still unwrapped! Karen felt that her father-in-law had pushed them to buy a house much larger than they needed. She knew that Jack longed for his dad's approval. The sad part was that Jack's dad seemed to praise, rather than caution, his son's expensive lifestyle.

After a year of agony and in desperation, Jack and Karen each hired their own lawyers and filed for bankruptcy and divorce.

✓ Spend some time thinking about Jack and Karen's situation. What do you think was the real cause of their problem?

✓ How would you describe Jack's attitude about finances? What role did Jack's dad play in this scenario?

✓ What advice about money would you give to Jack and Karen?

GODLINESS WITH CONTENTMENT

Many Americans, like Jack and Karen, find that spending becomes an uncontrollable force in their lives. The issue is not whether it is okay to enjoy nice things. The issue is a matter of control. Spending can be an unseen driving force that we use to mask all kinds of pain in life. Unfortunately it can also be a force that tears families apart and causes heartache and grief. Paul said, "But Godliness with contentment is great gain" (1 Timothy 6:6).

As I write this our country is in the worst financial crisis since the Great Depression of the 1930s. *But hidden below our national financial crisis is a spiritual issue.* What makes you feel good about yourself? What do you perceive gives you value or makes you happy? Is your relationship with Jesus enough to fill the longings of your heart? Or do you need more?

Mark 4:19 addresses this tension, with Jesus describing money as a deceitful thing that can choke out our spiritual life. Once again, if our walk with

God is solid, vibrant, and growing we then have the power to get control of our lives and our spending. Make your first financial goal to be content in Christ.

> *But the worries of this life, the deceitfulness of wealth and the desires for other things come in and choke the word, making it unfruitful.*
> —Mark 4:19

✓ Meditate on Mark 4:19 using the *Ask Questions* method. Jot down your observations.

Ask Questions

Is there:

A command to obey

A promise to claim

A sin to avoid

An application to make

Something new about God

Ask: Who, What, When, Where, Why

Emphasize:
Different words

Rewrite:
In your own words

✓ Use the *Emphasize Different Words* method of meditation and record your thoughts.

✓ Rewrite Mark 4:19 in your own words, and be prepared to share with the group.

✓ In Luke 12:15-21 Jesus describes a scenario of focusing on this world and not the eternal. What are your thoughts?

✓ What does it mean to be *"rich toward God"* in verse 21?

But godliness with contentment is great gain. . . . People who want to get rich fall into temptation and a trap and into many foolish and harmful desires that plunge men into ruin and destruction. For the love of money is a root of all kinds of evil. Some people, eager for money, have wandered from the faith and pierced themselves with many griefs. But you, man of God, flee from all this, and pursue righteousness, godliness, faith, love, endurance and gentleness.

—1 Timothy 6:6, 9-11

✓ Study 1 Timothy 6:6, 9-11. What are some of the warnings in this passage about money? List at least three.

1.

2.

3.

✓ What should a Christian's goal be from verse 6?

✓ Jot down a bad decision you have made with money. What did you learn from this experience?

Points to Remember

1. How we use and view money is deeply influenced by our parents and what we believe gives us value or makes us happy.

2. There is a tension between living responsibly in this world and having our treasure in heaven.

3. Money is deceitful. It can hinder our walk with God and cause us to try to get our self- worth from what we own or can purchase.

4. We must develop biblical values in the area of money. Otherwise we will be driven by the pressures of our society and the principles of this world.

✓ Reread the *Points to Remember.* Then jot down your thoughts as to whether you agree or disagree. Why?

✓ Why is 1 Timothy 6:6 called the anti-Weight Watchers verse? Because "godliness with contentment is_____ _____!"

Application to Curb Impulse Buying

1. Discuss with your spouse a decision that neither of you make an unplanned purchase over a designated amount ($100 or an agreed upon amount) without talking it over first. Men, make sure you model first any changes in your family finances. Do not expect your wife to make sacrifices that she has not seen you make.

2. When you are tempted to make a sudden purchase, place the decision on hold for one month. Mark it on the calendar. If, after thirty days you and your spouse have prayed and still feel peace about this purchase, then go for it. Most impulse purchases lose their appeal over time.

Financial Principle

There is no such thing as an independent financial decision. When you spend money on one item it means that you are excluding every other possibility for where that money could be spent. This is why impulse buying can have such serious consequences.

EVERY MAN A WARRIOR

ASSIGNMENT FOR NEXT WEEK

1. We will study the topic of money for the next few weeks. I suggest you use one to two Quiet Times doing the next lesson.

2. Have your next few Quiet Times on the suggested passages. These passages will help you grasp key biblical principles on the issue of money: Luke 16:1-13; Luke 16:19-31; Matthew 6:19-34; 1 Timothy 6:17-19.

3. ✓ Place Mark 4:19 in the front window of your *EMAW Verse Pack* and memorize it this week. Be prepared to review all your verses and share your Quiet Time thoughts with the group.

✓ End the group in prayer using the *WAR* method.

Leader's Guide to

LESSON 2
LIVE ON LESS THAN YOU EARN

NOTE TO NEW LEADERS

You can download the Leader's Guide from the website *www.EveryManAWarrior.com* to make it easier to follow while leading the lesson. It is important to follow the Leader's Guide while leading the lesson. While some items are the same each week, others are special, one-time instructions that will negatively impact the study if missed. These items are marked with a star. ★

LIVE ON LESS THAN YOU EARN

✓ Break into pairs and recite your verses to each other. Recite all your previously learned verses as well.

✓ Sign off on the *Completion Record.*

✓ Ask someone to open the session with prayer.

★✓ *Ask the men if they remembered to use the suggested passages on money from the assignment for their Quiet Times.* Encourage them to use these passages to help them develop a greater understanding of the topic.

✓ Go around the room, asking each man to share one Quiet Time.

✓ Begin reading the lesson paragraph by paragraph.

✓ Pages 20–30: Ask each of the questions on these pages. Depending on time, have two to four people give their answer. Try to include everyone.

✓ Page 25: Have each person read his summary on the danger and realities of debt.

✓ Pages 29–30: Read *Possible Applications*, the *Financial Principle, Points to Remember* and the *Assignment.*

★✓ Page 30: Point out that they should have their Quiet Times on the suggested verses.

✓ Page 30: Place Proverbs 22:7 in the front window of your *EMAW Verse Pack* and memorize it this week.

✓ End the group in prayer using the *WAR* method.

LIVE ON LESS THAN YOU EARN

Dan and Cheryl came to Christ during their college years. Dan proposed at the local Pizza Hut, where they were both working to put themselves through college. His unique proposal came by leaving a message on the employee's bulletin board where he had also asked for their first date.

The excitement of graduation, the upcoming wedding, and job searches were tempered by Dan and Cheryl's desire to live their lives wisely. When I first met Dan the summer after his graduation, I was amazed at his deep desire to learn and apply what the Bible said about money. The couple wanted to get married right away, but Dan didn't have a job, and they both had college loans to pay off. As we counseled together, one verse seemed to come alive for Dan: *"First you should work outside and prepare your fields. After that, you can start having your family"* (Proverbs 24:27 ICB). Dan began to see his vulnerability in getting married without having a job.

During the next few months Dan and Cheryl decided to delay marriage until they both had jobs and had paid off their student loans. When the big day finally came, they were totally debt-free and employed.

To avoid a major cutback when children arrived, they decided to live on Dan's salary and save Cheryl's for a house down payment. It was hard. Dan had an entry-level salary, and both their cars were old. But the cars ran fairly well, mostly due to Dan's Saturday routine of car repair and upkeep. Many of their college friends had gotten jobs, married, bought new cars, and generally lived more upscale lifestyles. In fact, their friends thought it strange that as DINKs (dual income, no kids), Dan and Cheryl still lived so conservatively.

Seven years later, Dan and three of his high school buddies kept their promise to take a two-week Alaskan vacation. All married for a few years, the other couples also had dual incomes. At night the discussions invariably turned to their jobs, homes, and the financial pressures they were facing. One couple had bought new cars and lived in an expensive townhouse, but were deeply in debt. They lived month-to-month on both salaries and had to pay for the Alaskan adventure on their credit cards.

Being willing to delay pleasure in the short run to gain financial freedom in the long run is a sign of maturity—and one of the most important financial lessons men can learn.

In their fireside chats, Dan and Cheryl smiled involuntarily as their friends shared their spats about who overspent the most or who had purchased more unneeded things. One couple felt that since they both had good jobs, they should buy whatever they wanted and figure out how to pay for it later.

Dan and Cheryl came home thankful for the tradeoff they had made. Their old cars and modest two-bedroom apartment had allowed them to save almost 50 percent toward the price of a home. They were debt-free and could start their family at any time. Dan had moved up to middle management since the company owner had noticed Dan's attitude of faithfulness both in personal finances and work.

As I considered the financial decisions Dan and Cheryl had made since college, some principles came to mind from our study on biblical financial management. One principle is from Galatians 6:7: "Do not be deceived: God cannot be mocked. A man reaps what he sows." Another is from Proverbs 22:7: "The rich rules over the poor, and the borrower is the slave of the lender" (RSV). We all reap the consequences of our financial decisions—good or bad! For Dan and Cheryl, their decision to avoid debt had given them a certain freedom that their friends had lost.

The rich rules over the poor, and the borrower is the slave of the lender.
—Proverbs 22:7 RSV

✓ Review the story of Dan and Cheryl. What thoughts do you have about how they planned their finances?

✓ How important is it for a couple to delay pleasure in the short run to gain greater financial freedom in the long run? Why?

Delayed gratification is a foreign concept to most Americans. Our culture teaches us that, *"We deserve the good life and we deserve it now!"* In 2006 some six billion credit card offers were put in our mailboxes—making the "good life" possible. But at what price?

Being willing to delay pleasure in the short run to gain financial freedom in the long run is a sign of maturity—and one of the most important financial lessons men can learn.

THE DANGERS OF DEBT

There is no place in the Scripture that says debt is a sin. But there are warnings about it, and it is always depicted as negative.

The world, however, says just the opposite. Most business schools communicate that debt is a good thing. Using OPM, Other People's Money, is taught as a way to prosperity and riches. With the principle of financial leverage working in your favor, the theory goes, you can quickly amass a fortune.

These OPM principles will work when the economy is going up, but they can be devastating when the market reverses. When an economic decline hits, another financial principle comes into play. In business it's called "last man standing!" This principle says that in hard times, those who are highly leveraged with little margin will go out of business.

As businesses are forced to sell, there is a glut on the market with too many sellers and no buyers. Those businesses that are out of debt lose less money and manage to survive. They also use this opportunity to upgrade their assets, many times for pennies on the dollar.

Financial leverage is when you put a small percentage down (say 10 percent) and borrow the rest.

We have all heard this: a man is highly leveraged with assets in the millions and boastful of his wealth. But with the first economic downturn he loses it all. A million dollars in assets does not make you rich if you owe $950,000—it just makes you vulnerable. And when asset valuations decline, it makes you bankrupt.

When times are good, be happy; but when times are bad, consider: God has made the one as well as the other. Therefore, a man cannot discover anything about his future.

—Ecclesiastes 7:14

✓ What are your thoughts on the use of OPM, Other People's Money, and financial leverage as a way to get ahead? How does Ecclesiastes 7:14 apply?

THE DANGERS OF DEBT

Look up the following verses, and jot down how they apply to money. Then answer these questions. Do you agree or disagree with the following statements? Why or why not?

✓ *Debt always presumes on the future.* James 4:13-17

✓ *Debt may deny God an opportunity to work.* James 4:2

✓ *Debt increases the stress on your life through the loss of freedom and increased worry.* Proverbs 22:7

FOUR PRACTICAL REALITIES OF DEBT

1. Personal debt lowers your standard of living. If you carry a balance of $5,000 on your credit card at 21 percent interest, you pay an additional $1,050 each year in interest.

For some it is not uncommon to have a running balance of $2,000–5,000 on all their credit cards. This running balance is equal to the amount of interest you will pay in only three and a half years. In other words, if you have a running balance of $5,000 on your credit cards, you will pay $5,000 in interest over the next three and a half years without even paying a penny on the principal! *Your standard of living goes down fast!*

2. Compounding works against you. Let's say you start with a $250 balance on your credit card at 21 percent interest and continue to overspend each month by $250. In five years you will owe $22,012. Now you want to pay this off. How much would you have to pay on this credit card each month to get rid of this debt in five years? Take a guess.

$366.87 $440.09 $595.50   My answer: $_____

Paying this debt over a five-year period means you will have spent a total of $35,730 with $13,718 in interest.

3. It is easier to get into debt than to get out. Here's the scenario. You over-spent by $250 per month to get into debt. Now you must not only stop over spending the $250, you have to pay back $595.50 per month. This means you will lower your standard of living by $845.50 per month.

4. Debt can set up a cycle of generational bondage to borrowed money. Many people who finance most of their way through college are just getting their college loans paid off when they reach their mid-forties. This is also the time when their children are ready to leave for college—and another generation of debt is created and repeated.

The opposite is also true. When one generation lives frugally, saves for the future, and trains their children well, they can launch their children into life with very little or no debt. This can be one of the greatest blessings you pass on to your children. *Putting these biblical principles into practice has generational implications.*

✓ Which of the above four principles most applies to you? Why? Be prepared to discuss with the group.

✓ Write a summary of the dangers and practical realities of debt. Be prepared to share your thoughts with the group.

FOUR PRIORITIES IN SPENDING
(SEE ILLUSTRATION ON PAGE 28)

After credit card debt is eliminated, nothing relieves financial tension more than having an emergency fund. A liquid emergency fund is one in which the money is easily accessible. Financial advisors recommend three to six months of living expenses in a money market, checking, or savings account. The loss of a job, for most people, is devastating. I recently talked to a friend who had a middle-management position for twenty-seven years. His company was bought out, leaving him unemployed for five months. The family's emergency fund allowed them to weather this financial storm.

An emergency fund helps in other areas as well: unexpected bills, car repairs, appliances that go out, and so on. When we were first married, on the morning of my wife's birthday we were busy with Saturday household chores. June was in the basement doing laundry. Suddenly I heard her yell, *"Lonnie, come down here quick!"* I raced downstairs to find oil running from underneath the washing machine.

"Do you think it's broken?" June asked hopefully. This machine was more than twelve years old and we knew we would need a replacement soon. I called the repairman. Being well-acquainted with our machine, he agreed that oil leaking from the transmission was not a good sign and he recommended replacing it. I trudged upstairs to give her the bad news.

Not knowing June had heard the whole conversation, I found her happily singing, *"Happy Birthday to me, Happy Birthday to me, Happy Birthday new washer, Happy Birthday to me!"* We were both able to laugh, but only because money existed in our emergency fund for such a scenario. Before we had an emergency fund, such a birthday would have been a depressing memory. As a newlywed couple, the financial pressure of an unexpected expense would have overridden any festivities.

THE FIRST TWO PRIORITIES
IN PERSONAL SPENDING ARE:

1. Eliminate high-interest debt.
2. Establish a liquid emergency fund.

It is best to target the debt first. It is also wise to set aside a small amount each month to build a liquid emergency fund. When these two areas are accomplished, they will give you more financial freedom than anything else that I have seen.

THE NEXT TWO PERSONAL SPENDING PRIORITIES CAN BE TACKLED AT THE SAME TIME.

3. Savings to spend.
4. Savings for long-term goals.

SAVINGS TO SPEND

Most of us try to live on a monthly paycheck. Most bills cycle on a monthly basis as well. Other expenses occur less frequently but still regularly—car and home insurance, family vacation, gifts, sports camp, school projects, family conferences, and such. Still others are more irregular and unforeseen—such as car repairs, medical bills, or broken home appliances.

Many people ask if they can combine their *Savings to Spend* and *Emergency Fund* money. This can be done if you know exactly what amount is in the emergency fund and determine not to borrow from it in order to purchase a non-emergency item. Most people keep separate accounts to avoid this.

Remember: Your *Emergency Fund* is for emergencies only and your *Savings to Spend* fund is for items that are actually in your budget.

SAVING FOR LONG-TERM GOALS

Money for "long-term goals" are funds not to spend. These funds are to pay for future goals such as retirement, college education, or the start-up cost for your own business. Savings for long-term goals should be done in long-term investment vehicles such as stocks, bonds, growth mutual funds, or real estate. We will talk more about this type of investment later. The illustration on the next page gives you a visual of the Four Priorities in Spending.

FOUR PRIORITIES IN SPENDING

✓ Study the illustration below. Is this a helpful way to look at spending priorities? Why or why not?

4 Long-Term Goals

3 Savings to Spend

2 Emergency Funds

1 Pay off High-Interest Debt

4. Long-term investments
- Diversify
- Savings Not to Spend
- Real Estate
- Mutual Funds

Goals
- Retirement
- College Education
- Starting a Business

3. Saving for Major Items
- Car Replacement
- Vacation
- House Down Payment

2. Emergency funds
- 3-6 Months' Living Expenses
- Easily Accessible

1. Pay off High-Interest Debt
- Can give an immediate 18–21 percent return.

Possible Applications

1. Make a budget! You cannot manage what you don't measure. A budget is "planned spending." It frees you to spend joyfully on what you have determined is your priority. When there is no money in the budget for an item, there is no decision to make. A budget worksheet is available on the website: www.EveryManAWarrior.com.

2. Total up all your debts. Make a plan to pay off those debts starting with the highest interest or smallest loan first.

3. Make a decision to not use credit cards. Research has shown that people who buy with credit cards will spend 15-30 percent more than when paying with cash. There is an emotional connection to your money when you pay with cash—you feel the money leaving!

Financial Principle

Being willing to delay pleasure in the short run to gain financial freedom in the long run is a sign of maturity—and one of the most important financial lessons a man can learn.

✓ This week you will write your own *Points to Remember* by reviewing the lesson and answering the following:

✓ What are the *Three Dangers of Debt* from the Scripture?

✓ What are the *Four Practical Realities of Debt?*

✓ What are the *Four Priorities in Spending?*

EVERY MAN A WARRIOR

ASSIGNMENT FOR NEXT WEEK

1. ✓ Keep having your Quiet Times on the topic of money. These four passages will help you grasp some key biblical principles on this issue:

1. Proverbs 13:7, 8, 11, 16, 18, 20, 22; 2. Proverbs 27:24-27; 3. Proverbs 21:3, 5, 6, 17, 20, 21; 4. Ecclesiastes 5:10-15.

2. Place Proverbs 22:7 in the front window of your *EMAW Verse Pack* and memorize it this week.

✓ End the group in prayer using the *WAR* method.

Special Note
If you find yourself in the situation of credit-card debt and have missed a payment, be proactive. Contact your credit-card company, inform them of your situation, and request a change in the interest rate. Many credit card companies will lower your rate dramatically in order to avoid your account going into default

Leader's Guide to

LESSON 3

PROSPERITY—
A BALANCED
PERSPECTIVE

NOTE TO NEW LEADERS

You can download the Leader's Guide from the website *www.EveryManAWarrior.com* to make it easier to follow while leading the lesson. It is important to follow the Leader's Guide in leading the lesson. While some items are the same each week, others are special, one-time instructions that will negatively impact the study if missed. These items are marked with a star. ★

PROSPERITY—
A BALANCED PERSPECTIVE

- ✓ Break into pairs and recite all your verses to each other.
- ✓ Sign off on the *Completion Record.*
- ✓ Ask someone to open the session with prayer.
- ★✓ *Ask the men if they remembered to use the suggested Scripture on money from the assignment for their Quiet Times.* Encourage them to use these passages to help them develop a greater understanding of the topic.
- ✓ Begin reading the lesson paragraph by paragraph.
- ✓ Page 32: Ask one person to read each verse in the section, *What Determines Prosperity* and then share his title.
- ✓ Pages 32–38: Ask each of the questions on these pages. Depending on time, have two to four people give their answer. Try to include everyone.
- ✓ Page 33: Ask each man to read his summary on money.
- ✓ Pages 34–37: Read the *Four Principles for Investing.* Ask them, *"What did you learn?"* or *"What are your thoughts?"* after each principle.

✓ Page 37: Read the *Possible Applications,* the *Points to Remember* and the *Financial Principle.* Ask for questions or comments.

✓ Page 38: Read the *Assignment* and *Special Note.*

✓ Page 38: Place Ecclesiastes 11:2 in the front window of your *EMAW Verse Pack* and memorize it this week.

✓ End the group in prayer using the *WAR* method.

Prosperity— A Balanced Perspective

Everyone wishes they had more money. Some churches make God blessing your finances a major theme. Some teachers say that God is obligated to bless you if a certain formula of giving and faith is applied. *Is this really what the Bible teaches on money and how to get ahead financially?*

With over 2,000 references to money in the Scriptures, the Bible has a lot more to say about finances than just the topics of giving, faith, or trusting God. These themes are scriptural, but let's go deeper and see what else the Bible says about prosperity and wise money management.

What Determines Prosperity

✓ Look up the verses listed on the left. Draw a line from the verse to the proper title or description on the right side. *Use an NIV Bible if possible.*

Verse	Title or Description
Proverbs 22:7	Plan Well
Proverbs 21:17	Avoid Debt
Proverbs 14:23	Manage Your Assets
Proverbs 27:23	Be Diversified
Proverbs 23:20-21	Don't Live Extravagantly
Ecclesiastes 11:1-2,6	Stay Out of Sinful Behavior
Proverbs 3:9-10; 11:24-25	Give Generously
Proverbs 21:5; 14:8	Work Hard

The Bible teaches that many factors determine whether or not you will financially succeed. The Christians I know who do well financially give generously and trust God. But they also manage their money well, work hard, avoid debt, and live more modestly than they have to. *Giving attention to all these areas allows you to prosper. Each is important.*

✓ Choose your favorite three verses from the previous exercise. Meditate on each and jot down your thoughts on money.

Verse 1: _____ Thoughts:

Verse 2: _____ Thoughts:

Verse 3: _____ Thoughts:

✓ Meditate on the following verses and answer this question: As a Christian, what should be our goal with money?

Luke 16:9-13

Hebrews 13:5

1 Timothy 5:8

1 Timothy 6:6-11

1 Timothy 6:17-19

✓ *Review all the verses on pages 32-33.* Write a summary on what you have learned about money. Be prepared to share with the group.

Four Principles for Investing

It is the responsibility of every man to provide for his family (see 1 Timothy 5:8). God created us to do this, and there is a certain satisfaction in meeting this challenge and succeeding. In the next few pages we are going to examine a few financial principles that can help you succeed. "The plans of the diligent lead to profit as surely as haste leads to poverty" (Proverbs 21:5).

The following pages have more to do with our long-term goals, such as saving for college or retirement. We all need to plan for the future. Many people use the stock market or mutual funds to accomplish this. To invest in the stock market you need to have a seven to ten-year perspective. If you may need to access this money before that time, use another investment option.

Principle 1: Get Started as Soon as Possible

Get Started: The first lesson in growing wealth is to get started as soon as possible. For example: What will I need to save each month with a 12 percent return on investment, in order to have a $200,000 retirement fund at age sixty-five?

He who gathers money little by little makes it grow.

—*Proverbs 13:11*

If you start at:
  Age 25—$21.72 per month
  Age 35—$69.09 per month
  Age 45__$231.30 per month
  Age 55—$949.78 per month

It is easier to do if you get started early!

✓ Discuss as a group.

PRINCIPLE 2: THE RULE OF 72

The Rule of 72: Take 72 divided by the interest rate to see how long it takes for your money to double.

EXAMPLE:
    At 8%, 72 divided by 8 = 9 years to double your money
    At 12%, 72 divided by 12 = 6 years to double your money.

Question: If you have $5,000 in an IRA at 8 or 12 percent, how much will it grow to in 36 years?

At 8% your money doubles every 9 years:

Start	Year 9	Year 18	Year 27	Year 36
I--------------------I------------------I-------------------I-------------------I
$5,000	10,000	20,000	40,000	80,000

At 12% your money doubles every 6 years:

Start	Year 6	Year 12	Year 18	Year 24	Year 30	Year 36
I-------------I-------------I-------------I-------------I-------------I-------------I
$5,000	10,000	20,000	40,000	80,000	160,000	320,000

This illustration shows the reward of having long-term investments in higher-yielding investment vehicles. A 12 percent return on investment from a mutual fund seemed low in the 1980s and 1990s. With the recent crash in the stock market, it seems high. This is why a seven to ten year or longer perspective is essential for stock market investments.

✓ Discuss as a group.

PRINCIPLE 3: DOLLAR COST AVERAGING

Dollar cost averaging is a system of putting a set amount, say $250, each month into a fluctuating investment such as a stock or mutual fund. As the price per share goes up and down, you will always buy more shares when the stock is lower and fewer shares when the stock is higher. This insures that your average cost per share will be lower than the overall price average of that stock.

✓ Discuss as a group.

Read the passage below and consider how it applies to the next illustration.

Cast your bread upon the waters, for after many days you will find it again. Give portions to seven, yes to eight, for you do not know what disaster may come upon the land.

Sow your seed in the morning, and at evening let not your hands be idle, for you do not know which will succeed, whether this or that, or whether both will do equally well.

—Ecclesiastes 11:1- 2, 6

PRINCIPLE 4: REDUCE YOUR RISK IN ANY MARKET WITH DIVERSIFICATION

Two investors, each with $10,000 to invest for retirement in 25 years (Percentages represent average yearly returns over 25 years)

INVESTOR A—Diversified Portfolio of $10,000 invested with $2,000 in 5 different investment choices:

Investment 1	#2	#3	#4	#5
$2,000	$2,000	$2,000	$2,000	$2,000
Lost all value	earned 0%	earned 5%	earned 10%	earned 15%
and became	remained	grew to	grew to	grew to
$0	$2,000	$6,773	$21,669	$65,838
				Total=$96,280

INVESTOR B—Non-Diversified Portfolio:

$10,000 lump sum investment, earning 8% interest grew to a total of $68,485

Even though Investor A did poorly with investments #1 and #2, he earned 40% more, or $27,795, using the diversified investment approach.

✓ Discuss as a group.

Possible Applications

1. Caution: Do not start investing in a long-term investment plan until you have all high-interest debt eliminated and an emergency fund established.

2. Since your home is also a long-term investment, accelerate your payments to get it paid off sooner. You will save interest and can use your former house payment to dollar cost average into another investment.

3. Avoid "get-rich-quick" schemes or investments. Investing in someone's new venture always looks good on paper before the business is started. They only turn bad afterward, when the assumptions made in the business proposal are seen to be unrealistic.

Points to Remember

1. Prosperity and financial success come from a combination of many factors, and all are important. To be good stewards, we need to understand and apply the basic financial principles of investing.

2. God wants us to also focus on contentment, being good stewards, providing for our families, and using our resources for that which is eternal.

Financial Principle

To invest in the stock market you need to have at least a seven to ten-year or longer perspective. If you may need to access this money before that time, use another investment option.

EVERY MAN A WARRIOR

ASSIGNMENT FOR NEXT WEEK

1. Try to have your Quiet Times in these passages on money. As you meditate, they will help you grasp some key biblical principles on this issue: Deuteronomy 8:1-18; Psalms 49:16-20; 1 John 3:15-20; Ecclesiastes 2:3-11.

2. ✓ Place Ecclesiastes 11:2 in the front window of your *EMAW Verse Pack* and memorize it this week. Be prepared to review all your verses and share your Quiet Time thoughts with someone in the group.

3. Come with your lesson finished and be ready to discuss.

✓ End the group in prayer using the *WAR* method.

Special Note
Becoming a better money manager is a process. It will take time. For some of you these financial concepts are new and the lessons have given you a lot of information to digest. It will take time to grasp, understand, and implement a wise, biblical financial plan. It took one couple I know seven years to get out of debt, establish an emergency fund, and start saving for retirement. After you have finished EVERY MAN A WARRIOR, you can come back to these lessons to study and continue to develop or implement your financial plan.

Leader's Guide to

LESSON 4
TAKE HOLD OF THE LIFE THAT IS TRULY LIFE

NOTE TO NEW LEADERS

You can download the Leader's Guide from the website *www.EveryManAWarrior.com* to make it easier to follow while leading the lesson. It is important to follow the Leader's Guide in leading the lesson. While some items are the same each week, others are special, one-time instructions that will negatively impact the study if missed. These items are marked with a star. ★

TAKE HOLD OF THE LIFE THAT IS TRULY LIFE

✓ Break into pairs and recite all your verses to each other.

✓ Sign off on the *Completion Record.*

✓ Ask someone to open the session with prayer.

✓ Go around the room, asking each man to share one Quiet Time from the suggested passages.

✓ Begin reading the lesson paragraph by paragraph.

✓ Pages 40–48: Ask each of the questions on these pages. Depending on time, have two to four people give their answer. Try to include everyone.

✓ Page 47: Read the *Financial Principle.* Discuss the question.

✓ Page 48: Read the *Possible Applications and Points to Remember.*

✓ Ask for questions or comments after each section.

✓ Page 48: Read the *Assignment.*

★✓ Page 48: Place 1 Timothy 6:18-19 in the front window of your *EMAW Verse Pack* and memorize it this week. You will have two weeks to get this passage memorized, but start on it right away.

★✓ Next week is the next *Proficiency Evaluation* and a week to get caught up. Finish any lesson you have not done and spend extra time on getting all your verses.

✓ End in group prayer using the *WAR* method.

Take Hold of the Life That Is Truly Life

Ben graduated from college in 1954. He had been discipled by The Navigators and wanted to live his life for the Lord. He had majored in what would today be termed construction science. His dream was to build houses.

But Ben had a dilemma: no money. So fresh out of college, he went to work for a contractor, saved his money, got married, and started a family. During the five years before starting his own business, Ben did something else. He studied every verse he could find in Scripture on being a good businessman and managing money. His Navigator training had taught him how to meditate on the Word and the need to put what he learned into practice.

Out of this study of the Scripture, he developed his convictions about money: first, the need to minimize debt, and second, the conviction to use his financial resources to advance God's purposes.

Ben determined he would start his construction company with the money he had saved and trust God to grow the business without the use of debt. The local lumberyard would carry Ben for ninety days. He hired one employee, used some outside contractors, and started his first house.

Out of this study of the Scripture, he developed his main convictions about money: first, the need to minimize debt, and second, the conviction to use his financial resources to advance God's purposes.

His faith was often tested that first year. *With his commitment to avoid borrowing money, would God provide?* God did—and that first year his company built three houses using only the "no interest" revolving account at the lumber yard. The business had survived.

The next year they built and sold eight homes, all without debt. By year seven his company had grown and had become increasingly efficient. He was now building fifty homes a year.

Ben was not living for building houses. He was living for the eternal impact he could have through his life, ministry, and giving.

Ben and I first met in 1985, when he was giving a seminar on "Running Your Business Biblically" at a weekend conference. We developed a friendship, and he mentored me in the area of money for the next few years. Once, during our time together he told me this story.

There had been a real estate boom and bust in his city. Since Ben had no debt, he was able to sell his homes considerably under what his competition did and still make a profit. Consequently, he had work when others were being forced out of business.

One of his competitors asked him to lunch and said, "Ben, I see that you build bigger and better homes than I do and can sell them at a cheaper price. How do you do it?"

Ben asked, "How do you finance the homes you build?"

The competitor responded, "Like everyone else, I guess. I go to the bank and get a construction loan, which I pay back when the house sells."

"With fees and interest, how much cost does this add to your home?" Ben inquired.

"About $10,000 per house," he answered.

When Ben told me this story, I was shocked. My mind was racing, calculating fifty homes per year with a savings of $10,000 per home. Ben's company was beating the competition by $500,000 per year—just because he grew into business with convictions about debt.

But Ben's story doesn't end here. During the years that Ben was building houses, he continued to study the Bible on the principles of business and giving. He taught these principles to other men and tested them in the crucible of the real world, his own business.

Ben was not living for building houses. He was living for the eternal impact he could have through his life, his ministry to other men, and his giving. Ben wanted to live for that which was eternal, and he gave half of all his income to support missionaries and their ministries. He also became good friends with the missionaries he supported and began to visit their ministries in South America.

In his late fifties, Ben began to take off during the three coldest winter months in his upper Midwest city to go to South America, where he taught "Managing Your Money Biblically" to hundreds of new believers in a number of countries. His seminar had now grown to a weekend conference. The missionaries were thrilled that their new converts could gain expertise in an area where most of them felt weak. In fact, Ben helped a number of these missionaries start living more biblically with their own finances.

Special Note
The above story is true and should stimulate your thinking. It is not true that every business can be started without debt. Some businesses are more capital-intensive, and very few men could save the money needed to launch these businesses. However, the impact on the bottom line of a business that is operating without debt and the advantage it has over competitors is real.

✓ Jot down three to four observations from the story about Ben.

✓ How does a man's understanding of biblical truth in the practical areas of life, such as finances, affect the success of the man?

TITHING

Over the years I have discipled millionaires, business owners, truck drivers, doctors, lawyers, farmers, computer programmers, and the list goes on. Regardless if the man is rich, poor, or middle-class, they have each discovered what Ben learned: the joy of giving and the privilege of collaborating with the God of the universe to build something that will last for eternity. This is one of the greatest secrets of being fulfilled, taking hold of the life that is truly life. (Read 1 Timothy 6:17-19 on page 45.)

There is a progression in a man's life that brings him to a maturity in Christ. One expression of that maturing process is his freedom in giving. Here's how the process looks:

Come to Christ. ⟶ Begin the discipleship process. ⟶ Develop your love relationship with God. ⟶ Make lordship decisions, committing every part of your life to Christ. ⟶ Take hold of the life that is truly life by choosing to live for that which is eternal.

Giving ten percent of your income to the Lord is a good goal. But many times it is taught in a legalistic way. Some people who know they cannot give a full ten percent settle for feeling guilty and don't even try to give.

Giving is tied to our ability to trust God and the available financial resources we have. Both have to come together in order to be generous. When I have helped newer Christians in giving, we first do a Bible study on the subject. Then we pray and they ask the Lord where He would have them start in their giving. Some start at two or three percent, others start higher and they increase from there. Over time, as their walk with God grows, their ability to trust Him matures, and their desire and capacity to give are also enhanced.

Giving should really be about the privilege of collaborating with the God of the universe, to invest in that which will last for eternity.

When a strong teaching on tithing as *an absolute* has been preached in some churches, I have seen a disturbing event. Sometimes a richer person has bragged to me about his fulfillment of the ten percent rule and communicated that if other people would just be obedient, they too would be blessed financially.

But across the aisle in that same church is a single mom with two kids, who makes $17,000 a year waiting tables. She feels ashamed and defeated because her $1700 tithe would mean she cannot feed her kids. It costs a rich person very little or nothing in his lifestyle to tithe. For the single mom, it costs her dearly.

I have found another teaching among Christians that concerns me. This teaching says you should just step out in faith, start giving ten percent and trust God to supernaturally take care of the rest. God may lead some people to do this, but I have seen others who tried this, expecting God to bail them out of their financial dilemma. When God let them crash, they ended up disillusioned.

As we learned in Lesson 3, prosperity is determined by many factors. I find much of the teaching on giving is too simplistic, based on some formula and centered on the end prosperity of the person. Giving should really be about the privilege of collaborating with the God of the universe, to invest in that which will last for eternity.

I think it is interesting that the New Testament has no mention of tithing, although the Old Testament teaches it clearly. The New Testament seems to sanction proportionate giving. In 2 Corinthians 8:12 Paul says, "For if the willingness is there, the gift is acceptable according to what one has, not according to what he does not have."

✓ What thoughts did you have in the above reading on tithing? Jot down two to three observations and be ready to share your thoughts with the group.

It is my experience that if we help people with good financial management, their giving goes up. Because if the 90 percent is not in order, the 10 percent is in jeopardy.

—*Jake Barnett,* Wealth and Wisdom, *NavPress, 1987*

✓ Do you agree with the above statement? Why or why not? Should we wait until we have our finances in order before we start giving?

✓ There are Scripture passages connecting giving and the blessings that God gives in response. Meditate on the following passages and jot down your thoughts on each as it relates to giving.

2 Corinthians 9:6-7

Luke 6:38

Malachi 3:9-10

✓ Where should we give? (See Galatians 6:6; Deuteronomy 15:11.)

✓ When should we give? (See Proverbs 3:9-10.)

✓ What does God expect from those He has blessed? (See Luke 12:48).

Command those who are rich in this present world not to be arrogant nor to put their hope in wealth, which is so uncertain, but to put their hope in God, who richly provides us with everything for our enjoyment.

Command them to do good, to be rich in good deeds, and to be generous and willing to share. In this way they will lay up treasure for themselves as a firm foundation for the coming age, so that they may take hold of the life that is truly life.

—1 Timothy 6:17-19

Ask Questions
Is there:
A command to obey
A promise to claim
A sin to avoid
An application to make
Something new about God
Ask: Who, What, When, Where, Why
Emphasize: Different words
Rewrite: In your own words

✓ Use the *Ask Questions* method of meditation on the previous passage. List all the *commands to obey*, and jot down your thoughts about how to apply these commands.

✓ Rewrite 1 Timothy 6:17-19 in your own words. Be prepared to share.

THE RELATIONSHIP BETWEEN A DONOR AND A MINISTRY

When you go to work each day you exchange your time, energy, and life for a paycheck so you can live. That's fine. But as Christians, our lives are not about the paycheck. It's about what we can accomplish with that income. Let's say that you make about $40 an hour and you send $100 to a missionary each month. You are literally sending two and a half hours of your life to that ministry. While God wants each of us to be ministering to others, you cannot give full time to witnessing, discipling other men, or feeding the homeless. But the missionary can. Every time he leads someone to Christ, disciples a man to walk with God, or feeds the hungry, you have, a part in that work. You exchange a part of your life for something that will last for eternity. Paul said in Philippians 4:16-17, "You sent me aid again and again when I was in need. Not that I am looking for a gift, *but I am looking for what may be credited to your account.*"

✓ What are your thoughts about the relationship between you as a donor and the ministries you give to?

Giving may not be about an amount or percent but, about what we value. As Christians mature, their values change. In the story at the beginning of the lesson, Ben made it his objective to give 50 percent of his income. I know of a number of other men who give 25-35 percent of their earnings to ministries, and some of them are not wealthy. They have simply come to a place in their walk with the Lord where they enjoy being generous and want to live completely for that which is eternal. *They have taken hold of the life that is truly life.*

Financial Principle on Giving

All giving is to God. We don't give to our church, some organization, or the pastor. We give to God and we look to God as our provider with our reward coming from Him.

✓ What thoughts do you have on the above financial principle? Do you agree? Why or why not?

Possible Applications

1. Reevaluate your giving. Ask God to give you the faith to trust Him to increase your giving. Cut out one luxury so you can give more.

2. Join the support team of a missionary at home or abroad. Add his name to your prayer list and pray daily for his ministry, family, and support.

Points to Remember

1. Our freedom in giving is one litmus test of our spiritual maturity. As we mature in our walk with Christ, our values change. Our desire increases to give and to collaborate with the God of the universe by investing in ministries that will change people's lives for eternity.

2. When we give to a ministry, we become partners in what God is doing through their ministry and lives. We give to God, and He rewards our giving in this life and the next.

EVERY MAN A WARRIOR

ASSIGNMENT FOR NEXT WEEK

1. We have one more week on biblical finances. Have your Quiet Times in these passages this week: Luke 12:22-34; Mark 12:41-44; Philippians 4:10-19; 1 Corinthians 9:7-14.

2. ✓ Place 1 Timothy 6:18-19 in the front window of your *EMAW Verse Pack* and memorize it this week. You will have two weeks to get this passage memorized but start on it right away.

3. It is a time to review and reflect. Do the *Proficiency Evaluation* for lessons 1–5. Try to fill in the answers without looking first. Then go back to find and check your answers.

4. The *Proficiency Evaluation* is designed to help you gauge your own spiritual growth. Lesson 5 is also a week to get caught up if you're behind. Finish any lessons that you have not done.

✓ End the group in prayer using the *WAR* method.

Leader's Guide to

THE GOAL FOR THE CHRISTIAN

NOTE TO NEW LEADERS

You can download the Leader's Guide from the website *www.EveryManAWarrior.com* to make it easier to follow while leading the lesson. It is important to follow the Leader's Guide in leading the lesson. While some items are the same each week, others are special, one-time instructions that will negatively impact the study if missed. These items are marked with a star. ★

THE GOAL FOR THE CHRISTIAN

✓ Break into pairs and recite all your verses to each other.

★✓ Ask the men if they finished any lessons they had previously missed. Sign off on the *Completion Record.*

✓ Ask someone to open the session with prayer.

✓ Go around the room, asking each man to share one Quiet Time.

✓ Begin reading the lesson paragraph by paragraph.

✓ Pages 50–56: Ask each of the questions on these pages. Depending on time, have two to four people give their answer. Try to include everyone.

★✓ Page 52: Read the *Application.* Spend some extra time on this question. Remind the group that these applications are confidential. Allow each man to share his objective and action steps. Encourage the men with how they are attempting to apply these studies to their lives.

✓ Pages 53–55: Ask the men how they did on the *Proficiency Evaluation* questions. Then go through each question.

★✓ Page 56: In lesson 6 we start a new skill. Each of you will write your own *Points to Remember.* This exercise will help you review the lesson and grasp more deeply the key thoughts that need to take root in you. Use a highlighter or underline key parts to facilitate writing your own *Points to Remember.*

✓ Page 56: Read the *Assignment for Next Week* and close the group in prayer using the *WAR* method.

THE GOAL FOR THE CHRISTIAN

One time I taught my Long Range Financial Planning Seminar to a Sunday school class. After class an older gentleman came up and wanted to talk about his situation. He was agitated and felt concerned that they were behind where they should be at his age. Church was starting and his wife was waiting patiently outside. As we exited the Sunday school room, he walked up to his wife and with a high-pitched, harsh tone he blasted her saying, "You need to learn to spend less money!" Gentlemen, that is not a good way to make application from these last few weeks! *Let any changes you make begin with you!*

You have just spent the last four weeks tackling some of the money issues that we as men face. In light of all we have talked about, I want to leave you with one final question. In the area of money, *"What should the goal of the Christian be?"*

AN OVERVIEW OF BIBLICAL FINANCES

Wealth and Money Before Sin	**Wealth and Money After Sin**
God created it: • And called it good. • For our enjoyment. • For our testing and development. • For us to co-labor with Him in living for the eternal.	Satan uses it as a source of: • Temptation and discontentment. • Ruin and destruction. • Greed and covetousness. • Deception to rob us of truth. • Inflating our ego and causing us to forget God. • Obsession to acquire wealth.

THE GOAL OF THE CHRISTIAN SHOULD BE FREEDOM AND VICTORY

Freedom to receive—1 Timothy 5:18.

Freedom to enjoy—1 Timothy 6:17.

Freedom to provide for ourselves—1 Timothy 5:8.

Freedom to give and be generous—1 Timothy 6:19.

Freedom to be content—Philippians 4:11-12.

Freedom from debt and debt-related stress—Proverbs 22:7.

Freedom to prepare for the future—Proverbs 21:20.

Freedom to leave an inheritance—Proverbs 13:22.

Victory over envy and comparison—James 3:14-16.

Victory over worry and anxiety—Philippians 4:6-7.

Victory over being driven to acquire—Ecclesiastes 4:7-8.

Victory over spending to find fulfillment—Luke 12:15.

✓ Jot down at least three observations from the two lists on the previous page. How did issues of money change before and after sin came into the world?

✓ Reread the section, *The Goal of the Christian Should Be Freedom and Victory.*

• Jot down the one area in finances where you want to have greater freedom.

• Jot down one area where you want to grow in victory.

✓ *Application:* Take some time to review the last four lessons. Try to come up with one major application you want to make. Jot down a plan with your actions steps.

Objective—I want to:

Action Steps—I will need to do the following action steps to accomplish my objective:

CLOSING THOUGHT ON MONEY

Let me leave you with one closing thought when it comes to being wise in the area of finances: Trust God! No matter what your situation, rich or poor, God is committed to take care of you.

Ecclesiastes 7:14 says, "When times are good, be happy; but when times are bad, consider: God has made the one as well as the other. ***Therefore, a man cannot discover anything about his future***" (emphasis added).

I emphasized the last sentence because it's true. Nobody knows the future, but we all know the One who holds the future in His hands. So in your efforts to manage well the resources that God has given you, relax, trust God and leave it in His hands!

✓ Turn to the next page and do the *Proficiency Evaluation.*

PROFICIENCY EVALUATION
MONEY

Try to fill in the answers without looking first. Then go back to find and check your answers.

✓ According to 1 Timothy 6:6, what should be our first goal when it comes to money?

✓ What is the warning for our spiritual life when it comes to money in Mark 4:19?

✓ There is no such thing as an "independent financial decision." Why is that? Explain.

✓ When we don't live on less than we earn, we fall into debt. What are three biblical dangers of debt?

✓ What are four practical realities of debt?

✓ What is financial leverage?

✓ What are the four spending priorities? List them.
  1.

  2.

  3.

  4.

✓ Being willing to delay _____ in the short run to gain _____ in the long run is a sign of _____ and is one of the most important financial lessons a man can learn.

✓ The Bible teaches that there are many factors that influence prosperity. List as many as you can.

✓ What is the "Rule of 72"?

✓ What is the benefit of "Dollar Cost Averaging"?

✓ Do you believe that *diversification* in money management is a biblical principle? Why? What verse do we know on diversification?

✓ To wisely invest in the stock market you need a time frame of _____.

✓ What are some of the pitfalls of teaching a ten percent tithing rule as absolute?

✓ Giving is not about the amount or a certain percent. It is really about _____ _____ _____.

✓ All giving is to _____. We don't give to our church, some organization, or the pastor. We give to God and we look to _____ as our _____ and with our _____ coming from him.

ASSIGNMENT FOR NEXT WEEK

1. Try to have your Quiet Times this week on these passages: James 1:1-12; 1 Peter 4:1-19; 1 Peter 2:18-25; 2 Corinthians 1:3-11. These Scriptures will begin to give you God's perspective on *Going Through Hard Times.*

2. Continue to get 1 Timothy 6:18-19 completely memorized.

3. Next week we change topics to *Going Through Hard Times.* Every man will face trials in life, and God has a plan with a purpose in suffering. Come with your lesson finished and ready to discuss.

4. In lesson 6 we start a new skill. Each of you will write your own *Points to Remember.* This exercise will help you review the lesson and grasp more deeply the key thoughts that need to take root in you. Use a highlighter or underline key parts to facilitate writing your own *Points to Remember.*

✓ End the group in prayer using the *WAR* method.

Leader's Guide to

LESSON 6
WHEN GOD WANTS TO BUILD A MAN

NOTE TO NEW LEADERS

You can download the Leader's Guide from the website **www.EveryManAWarrior.com** to make it easier to follow while leading the lesson. It is important to follow the Leader's Guide in leading the lesson. While some items are the same each week, others are special, one-time instructions that will negatively impact the study if missed. These items are marked with a star. ★

WHEN GOD WANTS TO BUILD A MAN

✓ Break into pairs and recite your verses to each other.

✓ Sign off on the *Completion Record*.

★✓ Ask the men to count and report how many recorded Quiet Times they have had since the beginning of the course. You should have fifteen recorded Quiet Times. You will need to average three recorded Quiet Times per week to complete thirty by the end of the course.

✓ Open the session with prayer.

✓ Go around the room, asking each man to share one Quiet Time.

✓ Begin reading the lesson paragraph by paragraph.

✓ Pages 58–67: Ask each of the questions on these pages. Depending on time, have two to four people give their answer. Try to include everyone.

★✓ Page 66: Have each man read his *Points to Remember.*

✓ Page 67: Read the *Assignment.*

✓ Page 67: Place James 1:2-4 in the front window of your *EMAW Verse Pack* and memorize it this week. *(1 Peter 4:19 is an optional memory verse.)*

✓ Page 67: End the session using the *WAR* method of prayer.

GOING THROUGH HARD TIMES

✓ Read the poem at the right.

Every man will face some form of adversity, trials, testing or suffering in life. In fact, it is promised. "I have told you these things, so that in me you may have peace. In this world you will have trouble. But take heart! I have overcome the world" (John 16:33).

In Book 1 of this course we signed a commitment to *"become the men God wants us to be."* The Scripture teaches that suffering, trials, and hard times are necessary to bring about real change in our character, our values, and how we live.

When God Wants to Build a Man

When God wants to build a man
And to skill a man
When God wants to mold a man
To create so great and bold a man
That all the world will be amazed

Watch His methods, watch His ways
How He hammers him and hurts him
With mighty blows converts him
And with trials shapes him

Only God understands
When his tortured heart is crying
And every breath is trying

How God bends but never breaks him
And with good intentions makes him
He uses whom He chooses

Then God shows His splendor through him

Author Unknown

There is an old saying: "Money doesn't make a man but reveals a man." But it's not the same with hard times. *Trials, suffering, and hard times do make a man and do reveal the core convictions and values of that man.*

In the next few chapters we will discover:

- God's purpose in trials.
- How He would have us respond to suffering.
- How God relates to us when we are hurting.
- How we should treat people facing their own challenges in suffering.

✓ Jot down your thoughts on the statement: *Trials, suffering, and hard times do make a man and do reveal the core convictions and values of that man.*

WHEN GOD WANTS TO BUILD A MAN

Bob was not raised in a Christian home. When his parents separated at an early age, he lived part-time with his grandparents. They took him to church, and his grandmother read him stories from the Bible.

During the turmoil of the Vietnam era, Bob was in high school and seeking answers to the purpose of life. A friend took him to hear a Christian speaker and he accepted Christ. In that moment, Bob was saved from a life of waste and purposelessness.

The next year Bob went to college and joined a campus ministry. He continued to grow in his faith, led a Bible study on campus, and wanted to live for that which was eternal. Bob's parents kept in touch but found his faith in Christ annoying. He was majoring in construction science which made his dad proud, since he too was a builder.

After graduation Bob started his own construction company. Having never received his dad's approval, Bob felt the need to prove his worth. He worked hard and his business grew. Within a decade he was the most successful builder in his town. Other contractors feared his competition. He enjoyed the success but was dissatisfied with the small projects of his local area. So Bob was excited when given a chance to build a much larger project in another state. He was headed to the next level in his career.

Bob moved his business and family 200 miles and started the largest project he had ever built, a $6 million shopping mall on the edge of a major metropolitan city. Within another five years, Bob's business had grown to 300 employees with multimillion dollar projects going on in four states.

Bob still taught an adult Sunday school class each week, sat on the church board, and gave generously. He openly shared that the secret to his success was the business being dedicated to God. Outwardly, things were great.

But Bob knew in his heart something was wrong. He loved his business, but he always felt a slight pang in his heart when he told others his business was dedicated to God. He knew he was neglecting his family, and Jesus was not really the center of his life. The business was!

In 1994, which began as the best year ever, a $13 million office complex and a $9 million mall renovation promised significant profits for his company. But Bob felt a strange development in his walk with the Lord. He wasn't hearing from God like he used to. His Quiet Times were hurried and inconsistent. No matter, he mused—he was giving huge sums to his church, and he still taught an adult Sunday school class.

One day God did speak. Bob was standing on the balcony of his business office, overlooking the construction machinery being prepped for the next job. God spoke to Bob's heart and in a still, small voice asked, *"You love this more than Me, don't you?"* The words felt like a knife in Bob's side.

A few months later on a Monday morning, Bob's secretary came in unexpectedly and said his bank's vice-president was on the line. Great, we should play golf, Bob thought. But they did not discuss a golf date, and the news was not good. The mall renovation account that had $350,000 was now empty. The job foreman was nowhere to be found. He had cleaned out the bank account and skipped town before several major subcontractors had been paid. Work on the project with more than 100 employees came to a halt.

A few weeks later, a second catastrophe exploded. The multimillion-dollar office complex had its funds shut off and the work stopped cold. The development owner and his wife were getting a divorce. Later it was discovered that Bob's construction manager and the owner's wife were secretly having an affair—and now the developer wanted nothing more to do with Bob's company.

In the first fifteen years of business, Bob's company had maintained an excellent reputation, had never been in a lawsuit, and had always paid their subcontractors on time. Now Bob's company could not pay its construction bills. Within a month, eighteen lawsuits from subcontractors were filed against the company and against Bob personally. Another project manager, smelling blood, stole company records and attempted to take over a third project himself, working directly with the owner behind the scenes.

One vendor was interviewed on TV claiming that Bob's company had extorted funds from subcontractors and did not complete projects. Filled with falsehoods, the interview ran three nights in a row. Bob was devastated, had trouble sleeping, and over and over in his mind kept asking, *Why, God, did You let this happen?*

Within a few months Bob's construction company spiraled down from a multimillion-dollar, multi-state company with 300 employees to just three employees, with no work and few prospects. Bob's company owned every bulldozer model Caterpillar made, plus trucks, tools, and countless other equipment. One by one the pieces of equipment were sold to pay off bills and settle the lawsuits. Bob and his family moved from living in a mansion into renovated government housing.

Most of the Christians around Bob and his wife seemed to disappear. Some asked what sin they had committed and were counseled to figure it out so that things would get better. A few church leaders decided it was best if Bob didn't teach his adult Sunday school class any longer.

Interestingly, it was during this time that Bob again began to hear God's voice. His voice was kind, full of grace, and without condemnation. While visiting with a Christian leader he was encouraged to *"turn worry into worship!"* It was this new focus that rekindled Bob's passion to spend time with God. It was during these times he spent in the Word, prayer, and worship that the Lord taught Bob some of His greatest spiritual truths and life lessons.

More than a decade has passed since Bob's time of testing. At the end of the ordeal, all the lawsuits were settled and bills paid. Bob moved to another city with his family, a pickup, and one small construction skid loader. And so he began to build his business again. Today, Bob and his wife have four children and six grandchildren. His business has fifty employees, and he has built churches, schools, college dorms, banks, and other kinds of commercial real estate in an eight-state area. Bob continues to be a leader in his church, supports a number of ministries, and is often asked to share his testimony of how God took him through the fire of testing.

In his testimony Bob shares how he had been spiritually bound up in trying to obtain his personal value from his business success or the income it produced. Bob often concludes his testimony with this statement: *"When you walk with God through the fires of testing, the only things that get burned off are the ties that bind you."*

✓ Write down at least three observations about Bob's ordeal. How do you think you would have responded to this trial?

Consider it pure joy, my brothers, whenever you face trials of many kinds, because you know that the testing of your faith develops perseverance. Perseverance must finish its work so that you may be mature and complete, not lacking anything.

—James 1:2-4

Ask Questions
Is there:
A command to obey
A promise to claim
A sin to avoid
An application to make
Something new about God
Ask: Who, What, When, Where, Why
Emphasize: Different words
Rewrite: In your own words

✓ Spend some time doing the *Ask Questions* method of meditation on James 1:2-4. Jot down your observations.

✓ Rewrite James 1:2-4 in your own words. Be prepared to share your rewrite with the group.

When God allows suffering or hard times to come into our lives, His purpose is to mature us, to help us grow up. However, this process can only happen if we respond to the crises by going to God with our pain and choosing to do what's right. Fighting with God by making bad choices when we are in pain, resolves nothing, extends the trial, and many times hurts those around us causing even more pain.

So then, those who suffer according to God's will should commit them-selves to their faithful Creator [go to God] and continue to do good [what's right].

—1 Peter 4:19

✓ Spend some time doing the *Ask Questions* method of meditation on 1 Peter 4:19. Jot down your observations. (Some translations use "good"; others use "right." The Greek word means "a course of right action.")

Ask Questions
Is there:
A command to obey
A promise to claim
A sin to avoid
An application to make
Something new about God
Ask: Who, What, When, Where, Why
Emphasize: Different words
Rewrite: In your own words

✓ Use the *Emphasize Different Words* method of med-itation on 1 Peter 4:19. Meditate on the words or phrases listed below. Jot down how these phrases im-pact the meaning of the verse.

suffer according to God's will

commit themselves

faithful Creator

continue to do good

✓ James 1:2-4 tells us what God is doing when we are suffering. What is it?

✓ 1 Peter 4:19 tells us what we should do when suffering. What is it?

Note from the author for those who went from Book 1 to Book 3:
1 Peter 4:19 is in your verse pack. It was used in Book 2. I encourage you to pull it out and memorize it along with James 1:2-4 this week. It is my favorite verse on how a real man should respond to suffering: "Go to God and do what's right!"

✓ Look up 1 Peter 4:1-2. Jot down how suffering purifies our purpose in life.

✓ Look up the following verses and answer the question below.

Matthew 16:27
2 Corinthians 5:10
Revelation 22:12

How does the promise of rewards when you face trials affect your motivation to *"go to God and do what's right"?*

✓ Answer the next three questions after reading the Letter from God.

Letter from God

My son,

When you are suffering, trust me. Trust me to do what's best for you. I measure things differently than you. I want what's best for your soul, what will give you spiritual rewards in heaven. Men measure what is easiest, what is free from pain, what gives them pleasure. I measure what will bring you the greatest joy, joy that will last, joy that is based on an eternal reward, joy that comes from knowing me.

God

✓ Record three to four observations on what God wants when you are suffering.

✓ What do men want when they are suffering?

✓ Why are they different?

Points to Remember

✓ Review the lesson, organize your thoughts, and jot down the most important points to remember from this lesson. Be prepared to share what you wrote.

1.

2.

3.

4.

Points that others shared that I want to remember:

EVERY MAN A WARRIOR

ASSIGNMENT FOR NEXT WEEK

1. Have your Quiet Times in the following passages: Isaiah 61:1-3; Luke 4:16-21; 2 Corinthians 1:1-11; Galatians 6:1-9; John 8:1-11. As you meditate, these Scripture passages will help you grasp some key biblical principles for the next lesson.

2. ✓ Place James 1:2-4 in the front pocket of your *EMAW Verse Pack* and memorize it this week. 1 Peter 4:19 is also in your verse pack. It is optional but I encourage you to memorize it as well.

3. Each of you will write your own *Points to Remember.* This exercise will help you review the lesson and grasp more deeply the key thoughts that need to take root in you. Use a highlighter or underline key parts to facilitate writing your own *Points to Remember.*

4. End the session practicing the *WAR* method of prayer. Pray about any difficult issues occurring in your lives.

Leader's Guide to
LESSON 7
THE WOUNDED WARRIOR

NOTE TO NEW LEADERS

You can download the Leader's Guide from the website *www.EveryManAWarrior.com* to make it easier to follow while leading the lesson. It is important to follow the Leader's Guide in leading the lesson. While some items are the same each week, others are special, one-time instructions that will negatively impact the study if missed. These items are marked with a star. ★

THE WOUNDED WARRIOR

✓ Break into pairs and recite your verses to each other.
✓ Sign off on the *Completion Record.*
✓ Open the session with prayer.
✓ Go around the room, asking each man to share one Quiet Time.
✓ Begin reading the lesson paragraph by paragraph.
✓ Pages 70–78: Ask each of the questions on these pages. Depending on time, have two to four people give their answer. Try to include everyone.
★✓ Page 74: Have each man read his summary on how God responds to hurting people.
✓ Page 74: Discuss the chart on Tony, Leon, and Brian.
★✓ Page 78: Have each man read his *Points to Remember.*
✓ Page 78: Read the Assignment. Have them place Matthew 11:28-30 in the front pocket of their *EMAW Verse Pack.*
✓ End in prayer using the *WAR* method. During the request prayer segment, encourage the men to pray about the lesson and any wounds they carry.

THE WOUNDED WARRIOR

Tony was raised in a Christian home but always felt that dad loved his older brother Jack more than him. Growing up, Dad seemed to constantly show a preference for Jack. No matter how hard Tony worked or whatever his achievement, Dad was more thrilled with Jack's accomplishments. The message was clear: *"Tony, you don't measure up."*

As an adult, Tony was critical of himself and those around him. At work, Tony seemed eager to point out the flaws in other people. At home, Tony had three children, two girls and a boy. He loved each of his children, but it seemed that while Tony enjoyed his daughters he felt disappointed and was critical of his son. When his son grew up, he moved away, hardly ever speaking to his dad.

Leon grew up in a small midwestern town, where his dad owned a car dealership. When Leon was in junior high, his dad went bankrupt. Everything changed. Mom had to go to work as a cook, and Leon's dad, filled with shame, began to drink. His parents fought constantly about money, and Leon found it best if he avoided going home. In his heart he felt sad and often said to himself, *"I will never let this kind of thing happen to me."*

When Leon went to college he came to Christ. But the feeling that he would never have anything drove him constantly. With a degree in architecture, he landed a good job. But always fearing financial failure, he also worked as a private contractor at home after hours. For years he worked seventy hours a week.

Leon, now in his sixties, has a big home in an expensive neighborhood and drives a Lexus. His three children have grown up and moved away. He rarely hears from them and wonders why they never call. He feels annoyed that his wife likes to shop and spend money so freely.

Brian grew up watching his dad drink. As he got older, Brian learned to stay away to avoid getting punched, slapped, or cursed at when his dad was drunk. Sadly, when Brian was not around, his dad gave the same treatment to Brian's mom. He saw her bruises but felt helpless. When Brian got to high school he discovered weight lifting and played football. He felt strong and tough.

Coming home late on Saturday night, he found his father drunk and out of control. But this time he had cornered Brian's mom and was holding a pistol to her head. Brian attacked his drunken father and pinned him to the floor. After disarming his dad, and overwhelmed with rage, he pointed the gun at his dad's head, yelling, *"Don't you ever hit my mom again or I'll kill you!"*

While at college, Brian came to Christ and his life changed. But over the years he discovered a deep conflict inside himself. He hated his dad, yet longed for the approval of other men.

He worked out at the gym extensively, and it was there he met Craig. Craig was kind, older, and easy for Brian to be around. They often worked out together and then went drinking. Once, after drinking too much, they went back to Craig's apartment and had a homosexual encounter. For Brian, it was the first time he ever felt close to another man. Brian has lived a homosexual lifestyle ever since.

THE WOUNDED WARRIOR

I was born in the 1950s. My parents, even though they struggled, remained married for fifty-three years and raised seven children. However, my children were born in the 1980s and were raised in a vastly different culture than my own. Since the 1960s, changes in our culture have caused devastating consequences to families and children. The downward spiral of our culture continues, and the people around us are increasingly broken or wounded. We know it is happening but feel helpless to make it stop.

God understands woundedness! In fact, Jesus started His ministry by stating that His job description was to heal wounded people.

Woundedness happens because we live in a fallen world. The wounds may be hidden, but are very real. They fester and become the lies we believe about ourselves or about God. These lies and wounds come from the messages we received growing up. They come from hurtful events or painful relationships that cut deep and leave scars on our lives. Over time, the lies become the truth in our mind. The lie then begins to shape us, drive our behavior, and many times cause destructive patterns.

It is especially important that as Christians we understand wounded-ness—because the world is filled with hurting people, and God wants to heal us and use us to heal others. It is also imperative that as men, we understand woundedness because many of us live with deeply wounded wives. Or, life has so wounded both partners that the marriage is a ticking time bomb waiting to explode on us and our children.

Most men hate to talk about emotions, personal trauma, hurts, or fears. In fact, most of us try to repress our wounds so deeply that we cannot remember where they are buried. The problem is, the wound and the lie associated with it can explode any time it is touched. This unseen trigger mechanism causes us to lash out and wound the people around us.

All of us have been wounded! We each need God's help and healing. Otherwise we pass our wounds on to the next generation.

✓ What do you think of the statement that we are all wounded? Do you agree or disagree? Why?

✓ Do you think it is true that if we do not allow God to heal our wound-edness then we are destined to pass those wounds on to our children and those around us? Explain.

Fortunately, God loves us too much to allow us to stay imprisoned in our pain. When we have the courage to face our wounds, God heals us. Then, in His great wisdom and grace, God takes our pain and allows us to partner with Him to heal others.

God understands woundedness! In fact, Jesus started His ministry by stating that His job description was to heal wounded people and set them free from the lies that imprison them.

In Luke 4:16-21, Jesus launched His ministry from His home in Nazareth. He was asked to read in the synagogue and chose Isaiah 61. After reading the passage, He states in Luke 4:21, *"Today this scripture is fulfilled."* It seems that Jesus saw Isaiah 61 as His job description.

Take some time to meditate on Isaiah 61:1-3, broken into phrases below:

The Spirit of the Sovereign LORD is on me, because
the LORD has anointed me to [job description]:

• preach good news to the poor, . . . sent me to
• bind up the brokenhearted, to
• proclaim freedom for the captives and
• release from darkness for the prisoners, . . . to
• comfort all who mourn, and
• provide for those who grieve in Zion—
• to bestow on them a crown of beauty instead of ashes,
• the oil of gladness instead of mourning, and
• a garment of praise instead of a spirit of despair.
• They will be called oaks of righteousness, a planting of the LORD for the display of his splendor.

✓ Choose two of the phrases above in Isaiah 61. Describe what they mean and how they affect your understanding of why Jesus came?

1.

2.

✓ How does God see hurting people? Look up the following and jot down your thoughts.

Matthew 9:35-36

2 Corinthians 1:3-5

✓ Review your thoughts on Isaiah 61 and the above two passages. Write a summary of how God responds to hurting people. How should we respond?

Review the stories of Tony, Leon, and Brian from the beginning of the lesson to fill out the following chart. List the: (1) emotional wounds they have experienced, (2) a lie each believed about himself or about God, (3) their compensation behavior, and (4) impact on the next generation.

Person	Emotional Wound	Lie Believed	Compensation Behavior	Impact on Next Generation
Tony				
Leon				
Brian				

✓ Leader: Discuss the chart above. Have one person share his answers for the first story (Tony), then ask what different thoughts others have. Discuss Leon and Brian in the same way.

WHAT TO SAY TO HURTING PEOPLE

Some Christians are uncomfortable with suffering. They convey that if you are suffering, then something is wrong with your walk with God. Actually, the opposite is true. John 15:1-2 explains *how God prunes us so that we can be more fruitful.* Read this passage from John.

> **I am the true vine, and my Father is the gardener. He cuts off every branch in me that bears no fruit, while every branch that does bear fruit he prunes so that it will be even more fruitful.**
>
> *—John 15:1-2*

Sometimes people unknowingly say hurtful things to already-hurting people. These kinds of statements don't help; they only rewound them, increasing their pain and forcing them to withdraw.

Ignorance makes many experts! If your intent is good but your content is bad, it still hurts the person you are talking to. It is better to not give advice on something you have no experience in.

What to Say to Hurting People
"I am so sorry!"
Or:
"I cannot imagine what you are going through, but
I am so sorry!"
Or:
"I am so sorry!
What can I do? How can I pray?"

Good Intent—Bad Content Examples

To a couple who has lost a child: "Well, God will use this for good in your life!"

To someone who has cancer: "Has all your hair fallen out yet?"

To someone who was abused: "Why can't you just get over it? What's taking so long?"

To a man facing bankruptcy: "Maybe there is some sin in your life that you need to deal with?"

To someone going through a long-term illness: "If you would pray more, you might get through this faster."

Sometimes the most important thing we can do is just listen and say nothing. "Rejoice with those who rejoice; mourn with those who mourn" (Romans 12:15).

✓ Can you remember a time when someone said something hurtful or something encouraging when you were going through a hard time? Jot it down.

• What was said?

• How did it make you feel?

WHAT DOES GOD WANT US TO DO WHEN WE ARE HURTING?

Come to me, all you who are weary and burdened, and I will give you rest. Take my yoke upon you and learn from me, for I am gentle and humble in heart, and you will find rest for your souls. For my yoke is easy and my burden is light.

—Matthew 11:28-30

Ask Questions
Is there:
A command to obey
A promise to claim
A sin to avoid
An application to make
Something new about God
Ask: Who, What, When, Where, Why
Emphasize: Different words
Rewrite: In your own words

✓ Spend some time meditating on Matthew 11:28-30. Use the *Ask Questions or Emphasize Different Words* methods. Record your observations.

✓ What does Jesus reveal about Himself in this passage?

✓ How does it affect the way you relate to Him?

✓ What does it mean to *"find rest for your souls"*?

✓ Use your meditations above to rewrite Matthew 11:28-30 in your own words.

✓ *Leader: The next three questions go together. Have one man share each of his answers to these three questions. Then ask the next person to do the same.*

✓ Spend some time thinking about a childhood event or family-relating pattern that painfully affected you. If nothing comes to mind, pray and ask the Lord for insight. Jot it down.

✓ What impact did this event have on you?

✓ Is there a false message that comes from this event or relating pattern that affects the way you view yourself or the way you view God? Describe it.

Points to Remember

✓ Review the lesson, organize your thoughts, and jot down the most important points to remember from this lesson. Be prepared to share what you wrote.

1.

2.

3.

Points that others shared that I want to remember:

EVERY MAN A WARRIOR

ASSIGNMENT FOR NEXT WEEK

1. Have your Quiet Times in the following passages: 1 Corinthians 9:19-27; Matthew 28:1-20; 1 Thessalonians 2:6-13; 2 Timothy 2:1-13.

2. Place Matthew 11:28-30 in the front pocket of your *EMAW Verse Pack* and memorize it this week.

3. Next week you will write your own *Points to Remember.* Use a highlighter or underline key parts to facilitate writing your own *Points to Remember.* This added review to write your own key points will increase your understanding of the material.

Leader's Guide to

MAKING YOUR LIFE COUNT

NOTE TO NEW LEADERS

You can download the Leader's Guide from the website *www.EveryManAWarrior.com* to make it easier to follow while leading the lesson. It is important to follow the Leader's Guide in leading the lesson. While some items are the same each week, others are special, one-time instructions that will negatively impact the study if missed.

MAKING YOUR LIFE COUNT

✓ Break into pairs and recite all your verses to each other.
✓ Sign off on the *Completion Record.*
✓ Open the session with prayer.
✓ Go around the room, asking each man to share one Quiet Time.
✓ Begin reading the lesson paragraph by paragraph.
✓ Pages 80–90: Ask each of the questions on these pages. Depending on time, have two to four people give their answer. Try to include everyone.
✓ Page 89: Have each person read their *Points to Remember.*
✓ Page 90: Read the *Assignment for Next Week.*
✓ Page 90: Place Matthew 28:18-20 in the front window of your *EMAW Verse Pack* and memorize it this week.
✓ End in group prayer using the *WAR* method. Spend some time praying about starting *EVERY MAN A WARRIOR* groups.

MAKING YOUR LIFE COUNT

Arlyn and Hannah were both executives at the same brokerage house in Seattle. Long hours and lots of travel caused each of their first marriages to flounder and eventually end in divorce.

Being good friends and coworkers with similar values, they thought they could make a relationship work and got married.

After a few years of the intense pressure of corporate life, they decided to make a change. They pooled their money, tendered their resignations, and decided to start their own business.

The coffee phenomenon of Starbucks had been born in Seattle. Arlyn and Hannah had watched, thinking it might be a new trend. They wanted to be on the ground floor of this new industry and moved to Omaha. Arlyn and Hannah started with a coffee kiosk inside the entrance of a major shopping mall.

Selling a $3 cup of coffee was a new idea in the late 1980s. The conservative nature of native Nebraskans, bred from pioneer stock, made it a challenge. But Arlyn and Hannah gave it their all. After three years and a steep learning curve, the new venture turned a profit.

Over the next few years they opened a dozen stores around the city. With a growing demand for the robust taste of high-end coffees and the addition of wireless Internet, their stores became a place for people to meet, students to study, and executives to do business over the aromatic brew. By the mid 1990s, Arlyn and Hannah's new venture was a smashing success.

Although successful, they were aware their lives were void of true peace and purpose. Now in their fifties, they decided to try church. Within six months they both gave their lives to Christ. About a year after this decision I met them, and they agreed to join me in a discipleship Bible study. They threw themselves into the discipleship process with the same zeal that had started their business. Arlyn and Hannah had succeeded in the world and it had not brought them joy. Now spending time with Jesus, having Quiet Times, and meditating on the Scripture was an exciting daily adventure.

As Arlyn and Hannah grew in their love for Christ, their lives dramatically changed, especially how they viewed their seventy-plus employees.

Before Christ, when a problem worker surfaced, the employee was promptly let go. Now Arlyn and Hannah, who knew the heartache of living without Christ, began to view each employee as an individual with the same emptiness. They began to pray daily for their staff to find Christ.

When it was discovered that one employee had a drug addiction, the couple paid for him to attend a rehab program. They promised his job would be there when he got out, if he could stay clean.

When other workers had problems they listened to them and Arlyn and Hannah would politely ask, "Would you be offended if we prayed for you?" Most of their employees were college students and somewhat bewildered being on their own for the first time. They welcomed prayer, and many of them cried openly. Hannah was always there with her hugs.

The workers and store managers witnessed the transformation of Arlyn and Hannah. Arlyn started opening their weekly business meetings in prayer, and he gave generous bonuses at Christmas. One major change was the annual Christmas party, which was no longer laden with booze.

After the first twelve weeks of the discipleship study, Arlyn and Hannah started the second course on how to share Christ with others. Within a few weeks they had memorized the gospel message and began talking with their family and employees about how Christ had changed their lives. They continued to pray daily for their staff.

Their faith message was credible because Arlyn and Hannah had begun to model their Christian faith before they began to share. Arlyn and Hannah were happy; and they showed sincere love and compassion for their staff. Even though they demanded high ethical standards, their business was a fun place to work.

Over the next four years Arlyn and Hannah led two family members and four employees to Christ. Their love for God seemed to overflow to the people around them. Arlyn and Hannah beamed with joy, seeing God use their lives for something eternal.

Then it happened! Arlyn had not felt well in some time and was having severe headaches. An MRI revealed a rapidly growing tumor on the brain. He needed immediate surgery, and the test revealed what they had feared— it was malignant.

It had been just four years since Arlyn and Hannah had given their lives to Christ. With their training in discipleship, they had consistently spent time in the Word and prayer. Their love for God had grown significantly—and it was clear they would need Him now that they were facing the fight of their lives.

The employees were deeply concerned and at the same time somewhat curious. Would the God that Arlyn and Hannah so openly talked about make a difference? For the next two years the employees watched intently as Arlyn fought his cancer, first enduring the chemo and then the radiation. Arlyn lost weight but never his smile. He joked with employees how his looks had improved after shaving his head bald because of the hair loss. He was still a joy to be around, even though they witnessed firsthand his pain and physical deterioration.

After two years, it seemed like the cancer had been beaten. I resumed meeting with them each week for prayer, sharing Quiet Times and reviewing verses. So I was stunned when I got the call. Arlyn had suffered a seizure and was being rushed to the hospital. The cancer on his brain had returned and the seizure left him paralyzed on the left side.

During the next two years Arlyn was in a care facility. Physical therapy and another round of chemo with a cocktail of cancer-fighting drugs might still save his life. I went each week to read the Bible and pray with Arlyn. His mind and speech had been unaffected and within a few weeks he had gotten the personal story of each of his nurses and caretakers.

Once when we had our heads bowed closing in prayer, a young nurse came in. She was startled by our prayer posture and began to apologize. Arlyn just smiled, asked her to come in said, "Can we pray for you?" He already knew her story.

She had been rejected by her family because she was unmarried and had a child. Her daughter was now two years old and sick. She had just started working at the care unit and the insurance would not cover the child's preexisting condition. Arlyn knew she felt scared and alone.

Arlyn took her hand and began to pray. He prayed for her, her little girl's illness, and for her family to be reconciled. His heartfelt prayer touched her pain, and the young woman began to weep. In the next two to three minutes Arlyn prayed over every aspect of fear she was feeling. I felt privileged to see God's love flowing through Arlyn to her.

After six months at the care facility, Hannah planned a surprise birthday party for Arlyn. More than sixty people showed up. Most were employees from the coffee shops and others came from their church. It was a mixture of two extremely different groups of people all gathered around Arlyn. After cake and ice cream, one of the men from church asked if we could pray. We held hands—churched and unchurched alike—and together bowed our heads praying for Arlyn.

I had prayed many times with Arlyn and Hannah for the people working in their business. I was a bit concerned that they would feel uncomfortable holding hands with strangers and praying, so I looked up. To my surprise what I saw on the faces of these young people was a deep longing for truth. Most of them had their eyes open and were watching as people prayed. They had witnessed firsthand Arlyn's coming to Christ, his changed character, his joy and hope in the midst of pain. It seemed that many were longing for this same peace.

A few months later Arlyn lost his fight with cancer and went home to the Lord. His coffee stores were all closed for the funeral. About fifty employees sat together at the back of the church, showing their love and respect for this man.

Arlyn and Hannah had instructed the pastor to share the gospel message, which had so radically changed their lives. We all bowed our heads at the end of the sermon and were asked to raise our hands if we too, like Arlyn, wanted Jesus in our lives. Ten hands lifted at the back of the church.

Because of the way Arlyn had lived his new life in Christ, in his death, ten new people came to Jesus and eternal life in Christ.

✓ Why do you think Arlyn and Hannah were able to touch so many lives for Christ? Jot down three to five observations.

✓ What role did discipleship play in their fruitfulness?

MAKING DISCIPLES IN THE TWENTY-FIRST CENTURY

Arlyn and Hannah had been Christians for only eight years when he died, yet their lives touched many others and were responsible for some sixteen people coming to Christ. They had learned to walk deeply with God, prayed constantly, and loved people sincerely. Even though they had been Christians for a relatively short time, God had used them significantly for that which was eternal. *Their lives had counted for something eternal!*

We are closing down on the last few chapters of *EVERY MAN A WARRIOR.* Several months have passed since we read Lesson 1, Book 1 and discussed the Great Commission of Matthew 28:18-20 to *"go make disciples."*

The prologue also asked a question: *"When I die, will I have accomplished anything? Will I have made a difference?"*

I believe the command to "go make disciples" and the desire God puts in every man's heart to make his life count for something eternal are connected. I hope the following questions and commentary will lead you to the same conclusion.

> **Then Jesus came to them and said, "All authority in heaven and on earth has been given to me. Therefore go and make disciples . . . , teaching them to obey everything I have commanded you."**
>
> —*Matthew 28:18-20*

In the last words of Jesus from Matthew 28:18-20, His instruction to the Twelve was *"Go and make disciples!"* This is not a passive statement! This command is in the imperative form. As a command given to every believer, it is worthy of our best efforts. I believe it is also the answer to how we as men can make our lives count for something significant, something eternal.

In Book 1, we focused on discipleship, learning some of the most important things that Jesus taught His disciples. Jesus gave this definition for "making disciples" from the above passage: "teaching them to obey everything I have commanded you." But Jesus also taught on the subjects of suffering, money, marriage, and raising children. Books 2 and 3 have been dedicated to teaching you how to be skilled and successful as a man in these areas. *EVERY MAN A WARRIOR* is a modern-day application of "go make disciples" for the twenty-first century.

EVERY MAN A WARRIOR was designed to give you biblical foundations and the practical truth or principles to:

• Walk with God for a lifetime.
• Face hard times and come through them in a God-honoring way.
• Manage your money well in order to provide for your family, be generous with others and invest in the future.
• Love your wife and be the husband God wants you to be.
• Know how to train your children, speaking truth into their lives and launching them well-prepared into life.

EVERY MAN A WARRIOR was designed to "make disciples" of men in the twenty-first century. Now that you have these biblical foundations and practical skills in your life, they need to be passed on!

✓ At what level have the principles and biblical truths of this course fully taken root in you? 10 percent? 30 percent? 50 percent? 70 percent? *Circle one.* Do not be discouraged if you feel it is a lower percentage than you would like. Most principles of truth do not sink in and take complete root until you teach those principles to someone else.

✓ Jot down why you chose that percentage. Be prepared to share your thoughts with the group.

✓ If you are a father (or grandfather), do you want to be able to pass these principles on to your children and grandchildren? If you are single, do you want to pass them on to other men? Why?

If you feel that these principles have only sunk into you at a 10 to 50 percent level, you may not feel you can effectively pass them onto your children, just yet. Here's the solution. Lead a group of other men through this same material. Go make some disciples of your own. Leading a group of men through the discipleship process of *EVERY MAN A WARRIOR* will greatly enhance your ability to pass these principles and skills on to your children.

According to the Learning Pyramid we discussed in Book 1, *Teaching Others* grows your retention rate at 90 percent, and may be the most effective way to get these biblical principles into your life.

Do you want to make your life count for something that will make a difference in the light of eternity? Then *"go make disciples,"* and you will greatly help other men in the process.

SPIRITUAL MULTIPLICATION

When I have discipled some men over the years, their lives have dramatically changed. But what thrills my heart even more is that many times their children then walk with God. Their children did not inherit the scars Dad had before he came to Christ and began the discipleship process. When you walk with God and disciple other men, it can have a generational impact for a number of generations. Your life really can make a difference in the lives of people and even future generations.

> ✓ If you disciple six other men and they each have three children and those children walk with God, get married, and have three children each, how many people will your life have affected? _____ This could be the impact of one nine-month study.

> ✓ If those six men also lead *EVERY MAN A WARRIOR* studies with six men each all having three children, then what would the impact be? _____

This process is called spiritual multiplication and it really works.

Then Jesus came to them and said, "All authority in heaven and on earth has been given to me. Therefore go and make disciples of all nations, baptizing them in the name of the Father and of the Son and of the Holy Spirit, and teaching them to obey everything I have commanded you. And surely I am with you always, to the very end of the age."

—Matthew 28:18-20

✓ Meditate on Matthew 28:18-20 using the *Ask Questions* method. Jot down your thoughts.

Ask Questions

Is there:

A command to obey

A promise to claim

A sin to avoid

An application to make

Something new about God

Ask: Who, What, When, Where, Why

Emphasize:
Different words

Rewrite:
In your own words

✓ Rewrite Matthew 28:18-20 in your own words. Be prepared to share with the group.

And the things you have heard me say in the presence of many witnesses entrust to reliable men who will also be qualified to teach others.

—2 Timothy 2:2

✓ Read 2 Timothy 2:2. How many spiritual generations can you see in this verse? What are they? Remember Paul is writing to Timothy.

✓ What criteria did Paul describe for the men Timothy should choose? What kind of men do you think should be recruited to an *EVERY MAN A WARRIOR* group?

✓ Do you believe that Jesus wants us to "go make disciples" even in the twenty-first century? Why or why not?

✓ Do you think that *EVERY MAN A WARRIOR* could be used as a modern-day application of "go make disciples" in the twenty-first century? Why or why not?

✓ What concerns do you have about leading your own *EVERY MAN A WARRIOR* group?

Points to Remember

✓ Review the lesson, organize your thoughts, and jot down the most important points to remember from this lesson. Be prepared to share what you wrote.

1.

2.

3.

4.

Points that others shared that I want to remember:

ASSIGNMENT FOR NEXT WEEK

1. ✓ Place Matthew 28:18-20 in the front window of your *EMAW Verse Pack* and memorize it this week.

2. We will resume sharing Quiet Times next week. Have your Quiet Times in the following passages: 1 Thessalonians 4:3-8; Proverbs 5:1-14; Proverbs 5:15-23; 1 Corinthians 6:9-20.

3. These lessons have more reading. Use a highlighter or underline key parts to facilitate writing your own *Points to Remember*.

4. We are close to the end of the course. Spend extra time this week working on your verses in order to get all the course requirements signed off.

✓ End in group prayer using the *WAR* method. Spend some time praying about starting *EVERY MAN A WARRIOR* groups.

Leader's Guide to

LESSON 9
SEX
AND MORAL PURITY

NOTE TO NEW LEADERS

You can download the Leader's Guide from the website *www.EveryManAWarrior.com* to make it easier to follow while leading the lesson. It is important to follow the Leader's Guide in leading the lesson. While some items are the same each week, others are special, one-time instructions that will negatively impact the study if missed. These items are marked with a star. ★

SEX AND MORAL PURITY

✓ Break into pairs and recite all your verses to each other.

✓ Sign off on the *Completion Record.*

✓ Ask someone to open the session with prayer.

✓ Go around the room, asking each man to share one Quiet Time.

✓ Begin reading the lesson paragraph by paragraph.

✓ Pages 92–103: Ask each of the questions on these pages. Depending on time, have two to four people give their answer. Try to include everyone.

✓ Page 103: Have each person read his *Points to Remember.*

✓ Page 104: Read the *Assignment.*

✓ Page 104: Place 1 Corinthians 6:20 in the front window of your *EMAW Verse Pack* and memorize it this week. Because we are so close to the end of the course, this verse is optional.

★✓ Page 104: If you have a teenage son, schedule a father-son time to read and discuss this lesson with him.

✓ End in group prayer using the *WAR* method. Spend some time praying about your own battles with moral purity.

SEX AND MORAL PURITY

When a man falls in love, the hormones released shut down all the parts of the brain that relate to common sense.

—Author Unknown

Adam and Bev were both raised in Christian homes in a time when our culture still embraced a Christian worldview. They grew up before there was TV. Their lives consisted mostly of hard work and church activities. Their parents were committed Christians, and at a very early age Adam and Bev each gave their lives to Christ.

Adam and Bev lived just miles apart in a rural midwestern area and met for the first time at a regional church retreat. Adam was eighteen, Bev sixteen, and they were immediately attracted to one another. Adam had never had such an intense interest in a girl before and over the next two years, they courted.

Adam realized he was in trouble. He had never thought so much about a girl. His heart ached when they were apart. Bev too was feeling emotions and excitement that had never been awakened before. As their relationship progressed, the intensity of these feelings grew. Two years after their first date they were married. They had never loved or been interested in anyone else.

They had stayed pure during their courtship and the thought of their wedding night was a little frightening, yet was filled with a godly anticipation of being able to release the pent-up desire they had for each other.

Their wedding night was a little awkward, but during the next few days they learned. Adam could not believe the beauty of his wife's body. Her softness and curves brought a sense of holy awe. Her loveliness and form was so different from his own. They could lie together for hours, just caressing, exploring, and holding each other close. Clinging to Bev, Adam's heart felt a sense of refuge, rest, and completeness.

Bev too was overwhelmed by the new emotions exploding inside her. She longed for his touch. His gentle caressing brought bursts of desire inside of her, something she had never known. She wanted to reveal all of herself to him and gave herself with complete abandonment.

During the next few months, they discovered even more ways to bring joy to each other. Whenever they were separated, for even a few hours, their longing for each other became almost unbearable. When Adam had to leave on an overnight trip, they clung to each other, feeling something was being torn from their insides. That first year of marriage was the happiest time of their lives.

During their first year of marriage, unknown to Adam or Bev, an unseen act of God had unfolded. Inside the DNA codes of both their bodies, a biological trigger mechanism designed by the Lord to bring oneness had tripped. For Adam, the start was seeing his wife in all her nakedness and beauty; for Bev, it was his gentle touch and his words of love.

This mechanism was activated in both their brains on their wedding night. An unseen flood of life-bonding hormones, chemicals, and endorphins were released from their brains, hypothalamus, and sex organs. These biological and chemical agents reached a level many times more than normal. It was creating a *"God-designed glue"* between Adam and Bev that brought a oneness of their souls. In God's plan, Adam and Bev would be bonded together for life.

During the next ten years, Adam and Bev had four children. Adam started a business and became intensely aware of his need to provide for his family. Once on a business trip, another man showed him a pornographic picture. Adam was immediately repulsed. He had never seen a naked woman other than his wife. He only wanted Bev's image of beauty stuck in his brain. What he and his wife shared was something pure and beautiful. Anything else felt dirty.

Adam and Bev were married for seventy-two years. They raised four children and lived to see their great-great-grandchildren. As they aged, their

> ### Vasopressin—A Hormone
>
> - Predominantly in males.
> - Awakens by visual stimuli.
> - Released into the bloodstream and into the brain.
> - Creates an insatiable biochemical bond between two people.
> - Released during intimate male-female contact.
> - Causes a laser-like focus on the person you are being intimate with.
> - You see her and track her in your mind even when she isn't there.
>
> The oxytocin levels in a woman jump to five times the norm during sex, creating a chemical bonding between couples.
>
> —The Science of Sex

only care was to take care of each other. When Adam died at age ninety-two, Bev grieved and comforted her family. Her mind was still alert and clear. But something had been torn from her soul, and knowing that she was no longer complete, ten days later she died too.

FAST-FORWARD FIFTY YEARS

Max was born during the mid-sixties in Denver. His dad and mom divorced when he was only five. Max's mom had to work full-time, and so he was left alone for much of his childhood. His mom was overworked, tired, and sometimes harsh with Max. When Max was ten, his mom remarried, to a business executive who also worked long hours. Even though he treated Max well, they hardly spent any time together. Max hung out mostly with other boys from the neighborhood.

One day, rummaging through the garage, Max found a hidden box of Playboy magazines. He showed his friends and together they laughed and enjoyed their new sense of maturing manhood. In the coming years, whenever Max was bored or alone, he looked at the magazines, now moved to a hiding place under his bed. It relieved the boredom, and he enjoyed the fascination he felt looking at the naked beauties.

By the time Max was sixteen, he was already experimenting with the girls in the neighborhood. One girl in particular he regularly pushed into having sex with him. He never really felt bad about it. From the stories he had read and the pictures he had seen, he knew this is how women wanted to be treated.

Max was good looking, over six feet tall, slender, and athletic. In college the girls threw themselves at him. He joined a fraternity where drinking and sex were the norm. After getting his business degree and an MBA, he wanted to settle down. He decided it was time to marry, and at the time he was dating Judy, one of the most beautiful girls he had ever known. She would do. But Max still looked at pornography on a daily basis. It had become his constant companion.

Two years after their wedding, Judy became aware of the affair Max was having with his office secretary. This had not been the first. Shortly after their wedding, Max had an affair with one of his old girlfriends. Sex was something he wanted and could easily get, so why limit himself to one woman?

Max and his wife already had a son and so they stayed together.

I met Max fifteen years later. He and his wife had become Christians. His long line of affairs had stopped for a while. Pornography was still a daily ritual. Max came to me for help because his wife had just discovered his most recent affair. It had been with her best friend. Judy was ready to walk. Max kept saying, "It was just sex—it didn't mean anything!"

✓ Contrast the childhoods of Adam and Max. What do you see in how those years affected their lives? Try to jot down at least three differences.

✓ Why was pornography able to take such a powerful hold on Max?

✓ What do you think of Max's statement, *"It was just sex—it didn't mean anything"?*

UNDERSTANDING SEX

When the FBI trains agents in the art of spotting counterfeit money, they spend 98 percent of their time studying original, perfect bills. When an agent ultimately knows the genuine article, it is easy to spot a counterfeit.

It's kind of like that with the issues of sex and moral purity. Our culture is awash in a sea of moral and sexual confusion. We need to start by going back to the original design that God had. What many people now call love is counterfeit and twisted.

In God's plan:

- Men and women are created by God as sexual beings.
- God designed men to be sexually stimulated by sight.
- Women were made to be stimulated by touch and loving words.
- God intended that sexual stimulation be activated and developed only in the context of marriage.
- God designed certain endorphins, chemicals, and hormones to be released in our bodies during sexual stimulation.
- These chemical compounds were intended to create a lifelong bio-chemical, emotional, and spiritual bond between a husband and wife.

"God knew that it would take a supernatural bonding between a man and his wife to face the challenges of life together. The mystery of bonding in sex is an involuntary one; sex creates a bond whether we want one or not. That's why breakups are so devastating and emotionally damaging. There is no more ironic a phrase than the oxymoron 'casual sex.'"
—Paula Rinehart, *Sex and the Soul of a Woman*

The Courtship Process in an Age of Casual Sex

After coming to Christ, marriage is the most life-changing event in a man's life. This transformation process begins in courtship.

What's interesting in today's culture is that those who chose abstinence before marriage are considered odd, deviant, or stupid. For a man or woman to stay sexually pure before marriage takes courage and a deep walk with God.

Trust is a major building block for any good marriage. At some level, having sex before marriage erodes that sense of trust. Here's why: *Sex always gets stuck in the place where it was first started.*

For the young woman being pressured by her boyfriend to prove her love, there is always a subtle sense of being used and disrespected. After a breakup she feels discarded and abandoned. Something that should be precious and beautiful is lost. Her ability to trust a man is greatly diminished, and she brings these feeling of being disrespected, used, and the resulting resentments into marriage. When a woman measures out tiny bits of herself over time to men, there may be nothing left to give to her husband in marriage. Her ability to bond for a lifetime and enjoy intimacy the way God intended is lost.

For the man, casually engaging in sex changes the way he views women. They become objects for his pleasure—a conquest for his self-centeredness. Deep down he begins to devalue them. *This is just the opposite of God's plan—which is for him to cherish, protect, and show them honor.* He then brings this sexual selfishness into his marriage. Eventually his wife begins to resent his physical needs because she feels used rather than loved.

Sex without commitment causes a man to be imprisoned in a form of permanent adolescence. He does not need to grow up, be responsible, plan, or build something for the future.

The best way for a man to mature is to do battle with his sexuality—to harness the energy contained in his sex drive, using that power for a greater purpose. God wants to bring him to a point where he will use his strength to live for something bigger than himself—the building, care, and protection of a new family.

If a man gets his validation from the fact that a woman gives in to his selfish desire for sex, it is actually a sign of weakness. In God's design, a man does not go to a woman to obtain his masculinity. No, he brings his masculinity, strength, and self-control to the woman, offering it to her as a canopy of protection for her future.

✓ What are your thoughts about abstinence before marriage in our current culture?

✓ Do you agree that sexual experience before marriage will have negative consequences after you get married? If so, how might it affect the couple?

✓ What thoughts do you have about a man coming to maturity by doing battle with his sexuality in order to harness it? What greater purpose might God have for this drive?

✓ Look up the following passages. What do they say about sex outside of marriage?

Proverbs 6:26

1 Corinthians 6:18-20

1 Thessalonians 4:3-8

✓ Write a paragraph from the above passages about the spiritual and personal implications of sex outside of marriage.

PORNOGRAPHY:
A CANCER ON THE SOUL OF AMERICA

Pornography is now one of the largest industries in America. "The adult entertainment industry takes in more money in any given year than professional football, basketball, baseball, and hockey combined," according to The War Within by Bob Reehm.

Like Max in the previous example, continued exposure to pornography has devastating consequences on a man's ability to experience real intimacy.

> **Pornography**
>
> • A $57 billion-a-year business.
> • Twice as many adult bookstores as McDonald's in the U.S.
> • 11,000 X-rated videos are released annually compared to 500 Hollywood titles.
> • 86 percent of college men use porn on a regular basis.
> —Porn Nation—The Naked Truth by Michael Leahy

Wes was a pastor who came to me because of his struggle with porn. As a Christian he knew it was dishonoring to the Lord and it was keeping him from spiritual fruitfulness. It was also destroying his marriage.

As we prayed together, the Lord began to reveal the root of the problem. Wes's mom had been a harsh, angry woman. Growing up, there had been few nurturing moments. As Wes got older, some of her criticisms were degrading to him as a man, an attack on his sexuality.

Wes began to use porn in high school. These women never rejected him or attacked his manhood. Porn eased the pain of life and the criticism he felt from his mom. But other unseen values were also being formed in Wes.

When Wes came to Christ in college he was set free from porn for a number of years. Wes married a beautiful woman and they had four children, two girls and two boys.

But Wes could never really feel close to his wife or his daughters. Even though his wife was extremely attractive and kept herself in great shape, Wes always felt dissatisfied. Her body was nothing like the pictures he had fed into his mind. No matter how hard his wife tried to please him, she got the message that Wes

> "Continued exposure to pornographic material causes an inverse ability to experience real intimacy."
> —Michael Leahy, Porn Nation—The Naked Truth

was disappointed in her. After twenty years of marriage, Wes stopped making advances toward his wife and retreated into the world of pornography.

✓ What factors caused Wes to become addicted to porn?

✓ How did porn eventually affect his life?

Addictions are real! When you give yourself to something, you become a slave to that issue. If it is porn, it leads to some form of death: the death of relationships or the death of your ability to really love those closest to you.

✓ Look up the following passages. What life principles are stated in these verses?

Galatians 6:7-8

Romans 6:16

✓ What do the above two passages teach us about addictions?

Pornography is serious business, with far-reaching consequences. I hope every man reading this will sit down with his teenage sons to read and discuss the lesson and this issue.

Another horrible result of a porn addiction is that pretty soon it no longer satisfies. Many times porn becomes a stepping-stone to acting out this addiction with prostitutes or the abuse of children. If you have children, you need to take seriously the statistics in the box on the next page.

OVERCOMING THE POWER OF PORN OR A SEXUAL ADDICTION

I am not an expert on this issue. If you need more help, here are some websites of ministries that have a good track record of helping men in the areas of porn and sexual addiction:

> • 1 in 6 boys are molested.
> • 1 in 4 girls are sexually abused.
> • 90% of sexual predators are known to the family.
> • 75% of teen prostitutes and 80% of incarcerated women were sexually abused.
>
> —www.Darkness2light.org

- www.covenanteyes.com (Internet accountability.)
- www.restoringthesoul.com
- www.darkness2light.org
- www.sexaddict.com—Heart to Heart Counseling Center
- www.ohmin.org—Open Hearts Ministry (If you were sexually abused as a child.)

Every man will struggle with sex and moral purity at some level. Here are some practical tips on reducing the strength and frequency of sexual temptations.

- *Keep a strong walk with the Lord.*

- *Pray daily for the Lord's help and grace in moral purity.*

- *Memorize key verses on purity such as: Job 31:1-4; Psalm 119:9-11; and Psalm 101:2-3.*

- *Stay away from places you know are a source of temptation. Get a porn blocker for your computer. See www.covenanteyes.com above.*

- *When a thought of lust enters your mind, begin to pray immediately.*

- *If you see an attractive woman and your mind is tempted, begin to pray for her, her salvation, and her relationship with her husband.*

I want to close with a story. In an Eskimo village, each Saturday night the men would gather to bet on a dog fight between two equally matched dogs, one black, one white. The owner of the two dogs always bet last and always bet on the winner. Some weeks the black dog won, other weeks the white dog. Finally the men of the village persuaded the owner to tell them how he always knew. He explained, "I know which dog will win because the week before the fight, I feed the one and I starve the other." Moral purity is like that. As long as we live in this world there is a fight going on between our flesh and our soul. The winner is always the dog that gets fed!

✓ How does the above story relate to pornography? If nothing comes to mind, see Galatians 5:16-17.

✓ What is an application that you need to make from this study? Do you need to apply any of the above practical tips? Which ones and why?

Points to Remember

✓ Organize your thoughts and jot down the most important points to remember from this lesson. Be prepared to share what you wrote.

1.

2.

3.

4.

Points that others shared that I want to remember:

ASSIGNMENT FOR NEXT WEEK

1. ✓ Optional: Place 1 Corinthians 6:20 in the front pocket of your *EMAW Verse Pack* and memorize it this week. We are close to the end of the course. The last two verses are optional. Spend extra time this week working on your verses and signing off on all the course requirements.

2. If you have a teenage son, plan a time with him when you can sit down to read and discuss this lesson. Be prepared to report back how it went.

3. Have your Quiet Times in: Genesis 2:1-15; 3:17-19; Colossians 3:22–4:1; James 4:13–5:6.

✓ End in group prayer using the *WAR* method. Spend some time praying about your own battles with moral purity.

LESSON 10
YOUR WORK MATTERS

NOTE TO NEW LEADERS

You can download the Leader's Guide from the website *www.EveryManAWarrior.com* to make it easier to follow while leading the lesson. It is important to follow the Leader's Guide in leading the lesson. While some items are the same each week, others are special, one-time instructions that will negatively impact the study if missed. These items are marked with a star. ★

YOUR
WORK MATTERS

✓ Break into pairs and recite all your verses to each other. Sign off all that applies in the *Completion Record.*

✓ Ask someone to open the session with prayer.

★✓ Go around the group, having each man share his *Completion Record* results from the back of the book.

• Did they get all the lessons done?

• Did they quote all verses?

• How many Quiet Times did they record?

✓ If anyone did not accomplish the *Course Requirements,* encourage him to keep going. It is essential that each man have all the course requirements finished before he attempts to lead a group of his own.

★✓ Ask if any man was able to read the last lesson with a teenage son. Have him share how it went.

✓ Go around the room, asking each man to share one Quiet Time.

✓ Begin reading the lesson paragraph by paragraph.

✓ Pages 106–114: Ask each of the questions on these pages. Depending on time, have two to four people give their answer. Try to include everyone.

✓ Page 110: Review the *Scripture Memory Proficiency Evaluation.* Have someone share his answer to each Scripture Memory statement.

✓ Pages 111–112: Read the *Conclusions* together.

✓ Page 114: Read the *Assignment* together. Discuss how to stay accountable and encourage each other in Quiet Times.

✓ End in group prayer using the *WAR* method. Spend some time thanking God for the work He has done in each life through this course.

YOUR WORK MATTERS

The first time the subject of *"work"* is mentioned in the Bible is in Genesis 2. It is mentioned in almost the same breath as the creation of man. Read Genesis 2:7 and 15 below. (The verses between 7 and 15 are a description of the garden.) After God created Adam in verse 7, He immediately takes him to the garden and says, "Go to work, take care of it" (verse 15). Since the beginning of time, men and their work have been intrinsically bonded together. It's in our God-given design.

> **The LORD God formed the man from the dust of the ground and breathed into his nostrils the breath of life, and the man became a living being . . . The LORD God took the man and put him in the Garden of Eden to work it and take care of it.**
>
> **—*Genesis 2:7,15***

In Genesis 3, sin enters the world and the issue of work becomes a much harsher reality. Because of sin, man's workplace went from literally being a "Garden of Eden" to a jobsite filled with thorns, thistles, painful toil, and demanding great effort.

✓ In the book of Ecclesiastes, Solomon shares some of my favorite passages on work. Look them up and jot down what he says about work.

Ecclesiastes 2:24

Ecclesiastes 3:13

Ecclesiastes 9:10

✓ Work also has a number of negative realities for a man. Jot down your thoughts from the following verses that warn us about work.

Ecclesiastes 2:17-19

Ecclesiastes 4:4

Ecclesiastes 4:8

Ecclesiastes 5:15

Then I realized that it is good and proper for a man to eat and drink, and to find satisfaction in his toilsome labor under the sun during the few days of life God has given him—for this is his lot. Moreover, when God gives any man wealth and possessions, and enables him to enjoy them, to accept his lot and be happy in his work—this is a gift of God. He seldom reflects on the days of his life, because God keeps him occupied with gladness of heart.

—Ecclesiastes 5:18-20

✓ Read Ecclesiastes 5:18-20 and answer the following questions:

✓ Is it okay to enjoy your work? (verse 18)

✓ Is work part of what God intended? (verse 18)

✓ When God allows you to enjoy your life and your work, this is a
_____. (verse 19)

✓ How does it affect a man when he has a job he can enjoy? (verse 20)

✓ What have you observed happens to a man when he has a job he does not enjoy?

Whatever you do, work at it with all your heart, as working for the Lord, not for men, since you know that you will receive an inheritance from the Lord as a reward. It is the Lord Christ you are serving.
—Colossians 3:23-24

✓ Meditate on Colossians 3:23-24. Jot down at least three observations on how God wants us to look at our work. What is the promise to claim?

✓ Rewrite Colossians 3:23-24 in your own words. Be prepared to share.

Seeing work as something we do for the Lord is perhaps the greatest attitude-changer I have observed in prompting men to look at their jobs from God's perspective. Because we are at the end of this course, Colossians 3:23-24 is an optional memory verse. But I encourage you to memorize it as your key verse on how God wants you to see work.

Helping your sons and daughters get perspective on work as a positive and normal part of life sets them up to succeed. Many times when my kids were young and just getting started doing chores, they would complain. Sometimes I would say, "Okay, let's go do it together" and then we would talk while we were working. I would try to be an example of *we all have to work so let's have a good attitude, work hard, and try to have fun.* If your kids hear you constantly complain about work, they will pick up the same attitude. It can be a setup for them to fail at work.

✓ What would be some important messages on work that you want to communicate and model for your children? Jot down at least three.

1.

2.

3.

✓ Review the lesson, organize your thoughts, and jot down the most important points to remember from this lesson. Be prepared to share what you wrote.

Points to Remember

1.

2.

3.

✓ Continue on the next page with the *Scripture Memory Proficiency Evaluation* and the *Conclusions.*

EVERY MAN A WARRIOR
SCRIPTURE MEMORY PROFICIENCY EVALUATION

✓ Write the Scripture reference from your memory verses that matches the statement on the left. Try to fill in the answers without looking first. Then go through your verses to check your answers. Each verse is only used once.

Which verse says: **Verse Reference**

If you don't ask, you don't receive.   _____

Don't worry about anything, but pray about everything. _____

You will be successful if you meditate day and night.   _____

Discipline is not pleasant, but produces a harvest of righteousness. _____

Listen to the Word and do what it says.   _____

The Scripture thoroughly equips you for every good work. _____

The deceitfulness of wealth chokes the Word.   _____

If you borrow money, you lose your freedom.   _____

Spread your investments around to seven or eight places. _____

This is the first and greatest commandment.   _____

If you've got wealth, don't put your hope in it.   _____

Trials bring you to maturity so you lack nothing.   _____

Are you weary and tired? God's yoke is easy.   _____

Do you want to make your life count? Make disciples!   _____

FOR THOSE WHO HAVE DONE BOOK 2

If you do all the talking and don't listen, shame on you. _____

Fathers, it is your responsibility to train your children. _____

Grant your wife honor.   _____

If someone hurts you, pay him back with blessing.   _____

You, as a man, are out of balance and need a helper.   _____

The tongue has the power of life and death.   _____

When you suffer, go to God, and do what's right.   _____

Give up your life for your wife.   _____

CONCLUSIONS

On January 15, 2009, a U.S. Airways plane with 155 people on board ditched into the chilly waters of the Hudson River. The pilot, Captain Chesley B. Sullenberger, did a masterful job of landing the plane in the river. Then with great courage, he walked the plane twice, making sure that everybody got out.

The flight was downed after striking at least one bird upon takeoff from New York's LaGuardia airport. With the engines dead, the plane cleared the George Washington Bridge by less than 900 feet before gliding into the water. The governor of New York, David Paterson, said, "Captain Chesley Sullenberger is a heroic pilot. We have had a miracle on 34th Street; I believe now we have a miracle on the Hudson."

The news programs ran the story for a number of days and later Captain Sullenberger was honored by President Obama at a State of the Union address. He is truly an American hero!

How would you have handled such an emergency if you had been trained as a pilot? As I was discussing this question with my good friend Jim, also a pilot, he made this comment: "In a crisis, your training takes over. It's all about training at that point."

The Christian life is like that. When you and I get hit with a crisis, this statement is true: "In a crisis, your training takes over. It's all about training at that point."

Jim had a beautiful wife named Christa. They had both discovered discipleship in their fifties, and had come to love the Lord. Their desire to make their lives count for eternity was strong. Christa's children were grown and she was an upper-level manager in the medical field. I still remember one special lunch with Jim and Christa. She asked for my thoughts about leaving her job in order to give herself to growing in her relationship with the Lord and spending time working in various ministries. I was thrilled for her.

A few weeks later she gave notice, left her job, and began spending two to four hours a day with the Lord. It was during these extended times with the Lord that she heard His voice say, *"Christa, get ready. Come close to me now!"* She knew the Lord was preparing her for something.

Two years later, Christa was diagnosed with stage-four ovarian cancer, a deadly killer. For Christa, Jim's statement could not have been truer. *"In a crisis, your training takes over. It's all about training at that point."*

The one-year survival rate for stage-four ovarian cancer is in the single digits. Miraculously, Christa fought and beat back the cancer for a full three years. Before she died, Christa was able to see her son marry and her daughter deliver a second baby. Christa knew her grandson and held her first granddaughter.

But the most amazing thing was how Christa fought. Her attitude of thankfulness to the Lord was inspiring. People came to comfort her and almost always the tables got turned. *She ministered to them!* Christa's words and example took their focus off their own problems and put their focus on the Lord, the place Christa rested and found refuge. Those two years spending extra hours with the Lord in her Quiet Times had deeply and intimately connected her to Jesus.

There were lulls in the cancer treatment. During one of those breaks I got together with Jim and Christa. I asked Christa what the Lord was saying to her and she immediately responded, *"Come close to me now!"* She continued, "Tell people to get ready. Tell them to go deep with God in the good times so that they can walk with him during the bad times. Go deep with God now because the trials of life will come."

During the three-year ordeal before Christa went home to the Lord, she touched hundreds of lives. Even in pain, her thankfulness and love for Jesus radiated from her. Psalm 119:50, *"My comfort in my suffering is this: Your promise preserves my life,"* became one of her most-treasured and often-shared verse.

The Lord had prepared and trained Christa for the trial she was to go through. Because just as her husband Jim had said, "In a crisis, your training takes over. It's all about training at that point."

✓ *"Tell people to get ready. Tell them to go deep with God in the good times so that they can walk with him during the bad times. Go deep with God now because the trials of life will come."* What thoughts do you have about Christa's advice? How does it apply to you?

NOTE FROM THE AUTHOR

If you have finished this course, I commend you. This course took work, dedication, and perseverance. *You are truly a Warrior!* More than ever, it is my hope that *EVERY MAN A WARRIOR* has given you the training necessary to become the man God wants you to be and to walk with Him for a lifetime. It is true: In the trials of life or just the day-to-day grind, your training takes over. It's all about training at that point.

When this course ends you will lose the accountability structure of the group. This is dangerous, as the Enemy will work overtime to get you to slack off on your time in the Word.

One of the worst investments you can make is to have spent the last nine months developing your discipleship skills and then let those skills die from inactivity.

Some groups, which have run from September to May, meet every other week during the summer for accountability. They share Quiet Times, review verses, talk about their lives, and pray with each other. This can also be a time to plan and organize for starting groups the next September. It can also help some to finish all of the course requirements.

Investing in the lives of other men through the discipleship process is one of the most rewarding things a man can do with his life. Discipleship allows you to colabor with the God of the universe in bringing real-life transformation to the lives of other men.

Discipling other men will also mature you spiritually and prepare you to more effectively disciple your own children. Once you have led a group through the *EVERY MAN A WARRIOR* discipleship process, the habits of Quiet Time and meditating on verses become a more deeply engrained habit.

ASSIGNMENT FOR...

1. ✓ Optional: Place Colossians 3:23-24 in the front pocket of your *EMAW Verse Pack* and memorize it.

2. ✓ As a group, talk about an accountability structure that will help you in doing your Quiet Time, Scripture memory review, and prayer.

3. Continue to put *EVERY MAN A WARRIOR* into practice by:

- Growing in your love for God by spending time with Him. Keep recording your Quiet Times. Never lose sight of the first and greatest commandment.
- Meditating on the Scriptures daily, being careful to put them into practice.
- Loving your wife and training your children well. In both cases, always be a model for them to follow.
- Managing your money so as to be free, generous, and able to provide.
- Going to God and doing what's right when times are rough.
- Passing the discipleship process on to someone else.

Check out the website EveryManAWarrior.com *for future updates, to download additional Quiet Time Journal sheets, or to purchase a new Quiet Time Journal.*

✓ End in group prayer using the *WAR* method. Spend some time thanking God for the work He has done in your life through this course.

APPENDIX

Quiet Time Journal

Completion Record

About the Author

THE EVERY MAN A WARRIOR ICON

The EVERY MAN A WARRIOR icon is a symbol of a man's Quiet Time. God intended for you to be a warrior that worships the person of Jesus Christ. Your Quiet Time is a place of worship; but also a place to get ready for battle. Make it your objective to spend enough time with Jesus each day to do both; worship and prepare for war. Each is an important part of who you are as a man.

I Am a Warrior and I Kneel at the Cross

I kneel at the cross, battered and bruised, with blood on my sword and a shield that is used. My helmet is off, my face is scarred. I'm weary and tired. I'm a warrior and I kneel at the cross.

I am also a prince and a son of the King, with power and authority to rule. But instead, I give up my life to serve because I'm a warrior and I kneel at the cross.

I live as a light in a dark world of pain. I fight to set captives free from their prison and shame. I battle for truth and I count the cost. I'm a warrior and I kneel at the cross.

I reject the world with its brokenness and loss, because He died for me upon that cross. Now I have HOPE and a lasting reward. I'm a warrior and I kneel at the cross.

I'm coming home soon when my battles are won. To see my father's face and hear, "Well done my son. You are home at last, take your place at my side; because I chose you to be a warrior and you knelt at the cross."

Lonnie Berger

Date_____ Passage I Read Today_____

Major themes from all I read.

Ask Questions

Is there:

A command to obey

A promise to claim

A sin to avoid

An application to make

Something new about God

Ask: Who, What, When, Where, Why

Emphasize:
Different words

Rewrite:
In your own words

Best verse and thought for the day. (Write the verse & your thoughts.)

Communicate With God

W - *Worship Him*

A - *Admit Sin*

R - *My Requests*

Date_____ Passage I Read Today_____

Major themes from all I read.

Ask Questions

Is there:

A command to obey

A promise to claim

A sin to avoid

An application to make

Something new about God

Ask: Who, What, When, Where, Why

Emphasize:
Different words

Rewrite:
In your own words

Best verse and thought for the day. (Write the verse & your thoughts.)

Communicate With God

W - *Worship Him*

A - *Admit Sin*

R - *My Requests*

Date_____ Passage I Read Today_____

Major themes from all I read.

Ask Questions

Is there:

A command to obey

A promise to claim

A sin to avoid

An application to make

Something new about God

Ask: Who, What, When, Where, Why

Emphasize:
Different words

Rewrite:
In your own words

Best verse and thought for the day. (Write the verse & your thoughts.)

Communicate With God

W - *Worship Him*

A - *Admit Sin*

R - *My Requests*

Date_____ Passage I Read Today_____

Major themes from all I read.

Ask Questions

Is there:

A command to obey

A promise to claim

A sin to avoid

An application to make

Something new about God

Ask: Who, What, When, Where, Why

Emphasize:
Different words

Rewrite:
In your own words

Best verse and thought for the day. (Write the verse & your thoughts.)

Communicate With God

W - *Worship Him*

A - *Admit Sin*

R - *My Requests*

Date_____ Passage I Read Today_____

Major themes from all I read.

_____

_____

Ask Questions

Is there:

A command to obey

A promise to claim

A sin to avoid

An application to make

Something new about God

Ask: Who, What, When, Where, Why

Emphasize:
Different words

Rewrite:
In your own words

Best verse and thought for the day. (Write the verse & your thoughts.)

_____

_____

_____

_____

_____

_____

_____

_____

Communicate With God

W - *Worship Him*

A - *Admit Sin*

R - *My Requests*

_____

Date_____ Passage I Read Today_____

Major themes from all I read.

_____

_____

Ask Questions

Is there:

A command to obey

A promise to claim

A sin to avoid

An application to make

Something new about God

Ask: Who, What, When, Where, Why

Emphasize:
Different words

Rewrite:
In your own words

Best verse and thought for the day. (Write the verse & your thoughts.)

_____

_____

_____

_____

_____

_____

_____

_____

Communicate With God

W - *Worship Him*

A - *Admit Sin*

R - *My Requests*

_____

Date _____ Passage I Read Today _____

Major themes from all I read.

_____

_____

_____

Ask Questions

Is there:

A command to obey

A promise to claim

A sin to avoid

An application to make

Something new about God

Ask: Who, What, When, Where, Why

Emphasize:
Different words

Rewrite:
In your own words

Best verse and thought for the day. (Write the verse & your thoughts.)

_____

_____

_____

_____

_____

Communicate With God

W - *Worship Him*

A - *Admit Sin*

R - *My Requests*

_____

Date _____ Passage I Read Today _____

Major themes from all I read.

_____

_____

_____

Ask Questions

Is there:

A command to obey

A promise to claim

A sin to avoid

An application to make

Something new about God

Ask: Who, What, When, Where, Why

Emphasize:
Different words

Rewrite:
In your own words

Best verse and thought for the day. (Write the verse & your thoughts.)

_____

_____

_____

_____

_____

Communicate With God

W - *Worship Him*

A - *Admit Sin*

R - *My Requests*

_____

Date _____ Passage I Read Today_____

Major themes from all I read.
_____
_____

Ask Questions

Is there:

A command to obey

A promise to claim

A sin to avoid

An application to make

Something new about God

Ask: Who, What, When, Where, Why

Emphasize:
Different words

Rewrite:
In your own words

Best verse and thought for the day. (Write the verse & your thoughts.)
_____
_____
_____
_____
_____
_____
_____

Communicate
With God

W - *Worship Him*

A - *Admit Sin*

R - *My Requests*

Date _____ Passage I Read Today_____

Major themes from all I read.
_____
_____

Ask Questions

Is there:

A command to obey

A promise to claim

A sin to avoid

An application to make

Something new about God

Ask: Who, What, When, Where, Why

Emphasize:
Different words

Rewrite:
In your own words

Best verse and thought for the day. (Write the verse & your thoughts.)
_____
_____
_____
_____
_____
_____
_____

Communicate
With God

W - *Worship Him*

A - *Admit Sin*

R - *My Requests*

Date_____ Passage I Read Today_____
Major themes from all I read.

Ask Questions

Is there:

A command to obey

A promise to claim

A sin to avoid

An application to make

Something new about God

Ask: Who, What, When, Where, Why

Emphasize:
Different words

Rewrite:
In your own words

Best verse and thought for the day. (Write the verse & your thoughts.)

Communicate With God

W - *Worship Him*

A - *Admit Sin*

R - *My Requests*

Date_____ Passage I Read Today_____
Major themes from all I read.

Ask Questions

Is there:

A command to obey

A promise to claim

A sin to avoid

An application to make

Something new about God

Ask: Who, What, When, Where, Why

Emphasize:
Different words

Rewrite:
In your own words

Best verse and thought for the day. (Write the verse & your thoughts.)

Communicate With God

W - *Worship Him*

A - *Admit Sin*

R - *My Requests*

Date _____ Passage I Read Today_____

Major themes from all I read.

_____

Ask Questions

Is there:

A command to obey

A promise to claim

A sin to avoid

An application to make

Something new about God

Ask: Who, What, When, Where, Why

Emphasize:
Different words

Rewrite:
In your own words

Best verse and thought for the day. (Write the verse & your thoughts.)

_____

_____

_____

_____

_____

_____

_____

_____

Communicate
With God
W - *Worship Him*
A - *Admit Sin*
R - *My Requests*

Date _____ Passage I Read Today_____

Major themes from all I read.

_____

Ask Questions

Is there:

A command to obey

A promise to claim

A sin to avoid

An application to make

Something new about God

Ask: Who, What, When, Where, Why

Emphasize:
Different words

Rewrite:
In your own words

Best verse and thought for the day. (Write the verse & your thoughts.)

_____

_____

_____

_____

_____

_____

_____

_____

Communicate
With God
W - *Worship Him*
A - *Admit Sin*
R - *My Requests*

Date _____ Passage I Read Today _____

Major themes from all I read.

_____

_____

_____

Ask Questions

Is there:

A command to obey

A promise to claim

A sin to avoid

An application to make

Something new about God

Ask: Who, What, When, Where, Why

Emphasize:
Different words

Rewrite:
In your own words

Best verse and thought for the day. (Write the verse & your thoughts.)

_____

_____

_____

_____

_____

_____

_____

_____

Communicate *With God*

W - *Worship Him*

A - *Admit Sin*

R - *My Requests*

_____

Date _____ Passage I Read Today _____

Major themes from all I read.

_____

_____

_____

Ask Questions

Is there:

A command to obey

A promise to claim

A sin to avoid

An application to make

Something new about God

Ask: Who, What, When, Where, Why

Emphasize:
Different words

Rewrite:
In your own words

Best verse and thought for the day. (Write the verse & your thoughts.)

_____

_____

_____

_____

_____

_____

_____

_____

Communicate *With God*

W - *Worship Him*

A - *Admit Sin*

R - *My Requests*

_____

Date_____ Passage I Read Today_____

Major themes from all I read.

Ask Questions

Is there:

A command to obey

A promise to claim

A sin to avoid

An application to make

Something new about God

Ask: Who, What, When, Where, Why

Emphasize:
Different words

Rewrite:
In your own words

Best verse and thought for the day. (Write the verse & your thoughts.)

Communicate With God

W - *Worship Him*

A - *Admit Sin*

R - *My Requests*

Date_____ Passage I Read Today_____

Major themes from all I read.

Ask Questions

Is there:

A command to obey

A promise to claim

A sin to avoid

An application to make

Something new about God

Ask: Who, What, When, Where, Why

Emphasize:
Different words

Rewrite:
In your own words

Best verse and thought for the day. (Write the verse & your thoughts.)

Communicate With God

W - *Worship Him*

A - *Admit Sin*

R - *My Requests*

Date_____ Passage I Read Today_____

Major themes from all I read.

Ask Questions

Is there:

A command to obey

A promise to claim

A sin to avoid

An application to make

Something new about God

Ask: Who, What, When, Where, Why

Emphasize:
Different words

Rewrite:
In your own words

Best verse and thought for the day. (Write the verse & your thoughts.)

Communicate
With God
W - *Worship Him*
A - *Admit Sin*
R - *My Requests*

Date_____ Passage I Read Today_____

Major themes from all I read.

Ask Questions

Is there:

A command to obey

A promise to claim

A sin to avoid

An application to make

Something new about God

Ask: Who, What, When, Where, Why

Emphasize:
Different words

Rewrite:
In your own words

Best verse and thought for the day. (Write the verse & your thoughts.)

Communicate
With God
W - *Worship Him*
A - *Admit Sin*
R - *My Requests*

Date_____ Passage I Read Today_____

Major themes from all I read.
_____

Ask Questions

Is there:

A command to obey

A promise to claim

A sin to avoid

An application to make

Something new about God

Ask: Who, What, When, Where, Why

Emphasize:
Different words

Rewrite:
In your own words

Best verse and thought for the day. (Write the verse & your thoughts.)
_____
_____
_____
_____
_____
_____
_____
_____
_____

Communicate
With God

W - *Worship Him*

A - *Admit Sin*

R - *My Requests*

Date_____ Passage I Read Today_____

Major themes from all I read.
_____

Ask Questions

Is there:

A command to obey

A promise to claim

A sin to avoid

An application to make

Something new about God

Ask: Who, What, When, Where, Why

Emphasize:
Different words

Rewrite:
In your own words

Best verse and thought for the day. (Write the verse & your thoughts.)
_____
_____
_____
_____
_____
_____
_____
_____
_____

Communicate
With God

W - *Worship Him*

A - *Admit Sin*

R - *My Requests*

Date_____ Passage I Read Today_____

Major themes from all I read.

Ask Questions

Is there:

A command to obey

A promise to claim

A sin to avoid

An application to make

Something new about God

Ask: Who, What, When, Where, Why

Emphasize:
Different words

Rewrite:
In your own words

Best verse and thought for the day. (Write the verse & your thoughts.)

Communicate
With God

W - *Worship Him*

A - *Admit Sin*

R - *My Requests*

Date_____ Passage I Read Today_____

Major themes from all I read.

Ask Questions

Is there:

A command to obey

A promise to claim

A sin to avoid

An application to make

Something new about God

Ask: Who, What, When, Where, Why

Emphasize:
Different words

Rewrite:
In your own words

Best verse and thought for the day. (Write the verse & your thoughts.)

Communicate
With God

W - *Worship Him*

A - *Admit Sin*

R - *My Requests*

Date_____ Passage I Read Today_____

Major themes from all I read.

Ask Questions

Is there:

A command to obey

A promise to claim

A sin to avoid

An application to make

Something new about God

Ask: Who, What, When, Where, Why

Emphasize:
Different words

Rewrite:
In your own words

Best verse and thought for the day. (Write the verse & your thoughts.)

Communicate With God

W - *Worship Him*

A - *Admit Sin*

R - *My Requests*

Date_____ Passage I Read Today_____

Major themes from all I read.

Ask Questions

Is there:

A command to obey

A promise to claim

A sin to avoid

An application to make

Something new about God

Ask: Who, What, When, Where, Why

Emphasize:
Different words

Rewrite:
In your own words

Best verse and thought for the day. (Write the verse & your thoughts.)

Communicate With God

W - *Worship Him*

A - *Admit Sin*

R - *My Requests*

Date _____ Passage I Read Today _____

Major themes from all I read.

_____

_____

Ask Questions

Is there:

A command to obey

A promise to claim

A sin to avoid

An application to make

Something new about God

Ask: Who, What, When, Where, Why

Emphasize:
Different words

Rewrite:
In your own words

Best verse and thought for the day. (Write the verse & your thoughts.)

_____

_____

_____

_____

_____

_____

_____

Communicate
With God
W - *Worship Him*
A - *Admit Sin*
R - *My Requests*

Date _____ Passage I Read Today _____

Major themes from all I read.

_____

_____

Ask Questions

Is there:

A command to obey

A promise to claim

A sin to avoid

An application to make

Something new about God

Ask: Who, What, When, Where, Why

Emphasize:
Different words

Rewrite:
In your own words

Best verse and thought for the day. (Write the verse & your thoughts.)

_____

_____

_____

_____

_____

_____

_____

Communicate
With God
W - *Worship Him*
A - *Admit Sin*
R - *My Requests*

Date_____ Passage I Read Today_____

Major themes from all I read.
_____

Ask Questions

Is there:

A command to obey

A promise to claim

A sin to avoid

An application to make

Something new about God

Ask: Who, What, When, Where, Why

Emphasize:
Different words

Rewrite:
In your own words

Best verse and thought for the day. (Write the verse & your thoughts.)
_____
_____
_____
_____
_____
_____
_____
_____
_____

Communicate
With God
W - *Worship Him*
A - *Admit Sin*
R - *My Requests*

Date_____ Passage I Read Today_____

Major themes from all I read.
_____

Ask Questions

Is there:

A command to obey

A promise to claim

A sin to avoid

An application to make

Something new about God

Ask: Who, What, When, Where, Why

Emphasize:
Different words

Rewrite:
In your own words

Best verse and thought for the day. (Write the verse & your thoughts.)
_____
_____
_____
_____
_____
_____
_____
_____
_____

Communicate
With God
W - *Worship Him*
A - *Admit Sin*
R - *My Requests*

Date _____ Passage I Read Today _____

Major themes from all I read.

_____

_____

_____

Ask Questions

Is there:

A command to obey

A promise to claim

A sin to avoid

An application to make

Something new about God

Ask: Who, What, When, Where, Why

Emphasize:
Different words

Rewrite:
In your own words

Best verse and thought for the day. (Write the verse & your thoughts.)

_____

_____

_____

_____

_____

_____

_____

_____

Communicate
With God
W - *Worship Him*
A - *Admit Sin*
R - *My Requests*

_____

Date _____ Passage I Read Today _____

Major themes from all I read.

_____

_____

_____

Ask Questions

Is there:

A command to obey

A promise to claim

A sin to avoid

An application to make

Something new about God

Ask: Who, What, When, Where, Why

Emphasize:
Different words

Rewrite:
In your own words

Best verse and thought for the day. (Write the verse & your thoughts.)

_____

_____

_____

_____

_____

_____

_____

Communicate
With God
W - *Worship Him*
A - *Admit Sin*
R - *My Requests*

Date_____ Passage I Read Today_____

Major themes from all I read.

Ask Questions

Is there:

A command to obey

A promise to claim

A sin to avoid

An application to make

Something new about God

Ask: Who, What, When, Where, Why

Emphasize:
Different words

Rewrite:
In your own words

Best verse and thought for the day. (Write the verse & your thoughts.)

Communicate With God

W - *Worship Him*

A - *Admit Sin*

R - *My Requests*

Date_____ Passage I Read Today_____

Major themes from all I read.

Ask Questions

Is there:

A command to obey

A promise to claim

A sin to avoid

An application to make

Something new about God

Ask: Who, What, When, Where, Why

Emphasize:
Different words

Rewrite:
In your own words

Best verse and thought for the day. (Write the verse & your thoughts.)

Communicate With God

W - *Worship Him*

A - *Admit Sin*

R - *My Requests*

Date_____ Passage I Read Today_____

Major themes from all I read.
_____

_____

Ask Questions

Is there:

A command to obey

A promise to claim

A sin to avoid

An application to make

Something new about God

Ask: Who, What, When, Where, Why

Emphasize:
Different words

Rewrite:
In your own words

Best verse and thought for the day. (Write the verse & your thoughts.)
_____
_____
_____
_____
_____
_____
_____
_____
_____

Communicate With God

W - *Worship Him*

A - *Admit Sin*

R - *My Requests*

Date_____ Passage I Read Today_____

Major themes from all I read.
_____

_____

Ask Questions

Is there:

A command to obey

A promise to claim

A sin to avoid

An application to make

Something new about God

Ask: Who, What, When, Where, Why

Emphasize:
Different words

Rewrite:
In your own words

Best verse and thought for the day. (Write the verse & your thoughts.)
_____
_____
_____
_____
_____
_____
_____
_____
_____

Communicate With God

W - *Worship Him*

A - *Admit Sin*

R - *My Requests*

Date _____ Passage I Read Today _____

Major themes from all I read.

_____

_____

Ask Questions

Is there:

A command to obey

A promise to claim

A sin to avoid

An application to make

Something new about God

Ask: Who, What, When, Where, Why

Emphasize:
Different words

Rewrite:
In your own words

Best verse and thought for the day. (Write the verse & your thoughts.)

_____

_____

_____

_____

_____

_____

_____

Communicate With God

W - *Worship Him*

A - *Admit Sin*

R - *My Requests*

_____

Date _____ Passage I Read Today _____

Major themes from all I read.

_____

_____

Ask Questions

Is there:

A command to obey

A promise to claim

A sin to avoid

An application to make

Something new about God

Ask: Who, What, When, Where, Why

Emphasize:
Different words

Rewrite:
In your own words

Best verse and thought for the day. (Write the verse & your thoughts.)

_____

_____

_____

_____

_____

_____

Communicate With God

W - *Worship Him*

A - *Admit Sin*

R - *My Requests*

Date _____ Passage I Read Today _____

Major themes from all I read.

_____

_____

_____

Ask Questions

Is there:

A command to obey

A promise to claim

A sin to avoid

An application to make

Something new about God

Ask: Who, What, When, Where, Why

Emphasize:
Different words

Rewrite:
In your own words

Best verse and thought for the day. (Write the verse & your thoughts.)

_____

_____

_____

_____

_____

_____

_____

Communicate
With God
W - *Worship Him*
A - *Admit Sin*
R - *My Requests*

Date _____ Passage I Read Today _____

Major themes from all I read.

_____

_____

_____

Ask Questions

Is there:

A command to obey

A promise to claim

A sin to avoid

An application to make

Something new about God

Ask: Who, What, When, Where, Why

Emphasize:
Different words

Rewrite:
In your own words

Best verse and thought for the day. (Write the verse & your thoughts.)

_____

_____

_____

_____

_____

_____

_____

Communicate
With God
W - *Worship Him*
A - *Admit Sin*
R - *My Requests*

Date_____ Passage I Read Today_____

Ask Questions

Is there:

A command to obey

A promise to claim

A sin to avoid

An application to make

Something new about God

Ask: Who, What, When, Where, Why

Emphasize:
Different words

Rewrite:
In your own words

Major themes from all I read.
_____
_____
_____

Best verse and thought for the day. (Write the verse & your thoughts.)
_____
_____
_____
_____
_____
_____

Communicate With God

W - *Worship Him*

A - *Admit Sin*

R - *My Requests*

Date_____ Passage I Read Today_____

Ask Questions

Is there:

A command to obey

A promise to claim

A sin to avoid

An application to make

Something new about God

Ask: Who, What, When, Where, Why

Emphasize:
Different words

Rewrite:
In your own words

Major themes from all I read.
_____
_____
_____

Best verse and thought for the day. (Write the verse & your thoughts.)
_____
_____
_____
_____
_____
_____

Communicate With God

W - *Worship Him*

A - *Admit Sin*

R - *My Requests*

Date _____ Passage I Read Today_____

Major themes from all I read.
_____

Ask Questions

Is there:

A command to obey

A promise to claim

A sin to avoid

An application to make

Something new about God

Ask: Who, What, When, Where, Why

Emphasize:
Different words

Rewrite:
In your own words

Best verse and thought for the day. (Write the verse & your thoughts.)
_____
_____
_____
_____
_____

Communicate
With God
W - Worship Him
A - Admit Sin
R - My Requests

Date _____ Passage I Read Today_____

Major themes from all I read.
_____

Ask Questions

Is there:

A command to obey

A promise to claim

A sin to avoid

An application to make

Something new about God

Ask: Who, What, When, Where, Why

Emphasize:
Different words

Rewrite:
In your own words

Best verse and thought for the day. (Write the verse & your thoughts.)
_____
_____
_____
_____
_____

Communicate
With God
W - Worship Him
A - Admit Sin
R - My Requests

Date_____ Passage I Read Today_____

Major themes from all I read.

_____

_____

Ask Questions

Is there:

A command to obey

A promise to claim

A sin to avoid

An application to make

Something new about God

Ask: Who, What, When, Where, Why

Emphasize:
Different words

Rewrite:
In your own words

Best verse and thought for the day. (Write the verse & your thoughts.)

_____

_____

_____

_____

_____

_____

_____

Communicate
With God

W - Worship Him

A - Admit Sin

R - My Requests

Date_____ Passage I Read Today_____

Major themes from all I read.

_____

_____

Ask Questions

Is there:

A command to obey

A promise to claim

A sin to avoid

An application to make

Something new about God

Ask: Who, What, When, Where, Why

Emphasize:
Different words

Rewrite:
In your own words

Best verse and thought for the day. (Write the verse & your thoughts.)

_____

_____

_____

_____

_____

_____

_____

Communicate
With God

W - Worship Him

A - Admit Sin

R - My Requests

Date_____ Passage I Read Today_____
Major themes from all I read.
_____
_____
_____

Ask Questions

Is there:

A command to obey

A promise to claim

A sin to avoid

An application to make

Something new about God

Ask: Who, What, When, Where, Why

Emphasize:
Different words

Rewrite:
In your own words

Best verse and thought for the day. (Write the verse & your thoughts.)
_____
_____
_____
_____
_____
_____
_____
_____
_____

Communicate With God

W - *Worship Him*

A - *Admit Sin*

R - *My Requests*

Date_____ Passage I Read Today_____
Major themes from all I read.
_____
_____
_____

Ask Questions

Is there:

A command to obey

A promise to claim

A sin to avoid

An application to make

Something new about God

Ask: Who, What, When, Where, Why

Emphasize:
Different words

Rewrite:
In your own words

Best verse and thought for the day. (Write the verse & your thoughts.)
_____
_____
_____
_____
_____
_____
_____
_____
_____

Communicate With God

W - *Worship Him*

A - *Admit Sin*

R - *My Requests*

Completion Record
Course Requirements for Book 3

This course is designed for men who want to become the man God wants them to be. Change will only happen when we do the work and give it our best effort. The *Completion Record* is a tool designed to help you gauge your progress and help you encourage each other to succeed.

Have another member of your group check you on the requirements of this course. Have them initial and date each item.

Scripture Memory Record

I have memorized and quoted word-perfect:

INITIAL – DATE

Mark 4:19 _____

Proverbs 22:7 _____

Ecclesiastes 11:2 _____

1 Timothy 6:18-19 _____

James 1:2-4 _____

Matthew 11:28-30 _____

Matthew 28:18-20 _____

1 Peter 4:19 (optional) _____

1 Corinthians 6:20 (optional) _____

Colossians 3:23-24 (optional) _____

Quiet Time Journal Record

INITIAL – DATE

I have recorded ten Quiet Time sessions in my journal. _____

I have recorded thirty Quiet Time sessions in my journal. _____

Book 3:
Money, Sex, Work, Hard Times, Making Your Life Count

INITIAL - DATE

Lesson 1: *Money and Contentment* _____

Lesson 2: *Live on Less Than You Earn* _____

Lesson 3: *Prosperity—A Balanced Perspective* _____

Lesson 4: *Take Hold of the Life That Is Truly Life* _____

Lesson 5: *The Goal for the Christian* _____

Lesson 6: *When God Wants to Build a Man* _____

Lesson 7: *The Wounded Warrior* _____

Lesson 8: *Making Your Life Count* _____

Lesson 9: *Sex and Moral Purity* _____

Lesson 10: *Your Work Matters* _____

Course Requirements for Completion of Book 3

INITIAL - DATE

• Finish all ten lessons _____

• Memorize and quote seven Scripture passages _____

• Recorded thirty Quiet Times or more _____

Congratulations! If you have finished this course with every item in the Completion Record checked off, you are to be commended. This course took work, dedication, and perseverance. *You are truly a warrior!* Download your Certificate of Completion from the website *www.EveryManAWarrior.com.*

ABOUT THE AUTHOR:
LONNIE BERGER

Lonnie Berger has been on staff with The Navigators, an international Christian organization known for its expertise in discipleship and leadership development, for more than 30 years.

While in college at Kansas State University in Manhattan, Kansas, Mr. Berger received his initial Navigator ministry training. His first staff assignment was behind the Iron Curtain in communist Romania, where he lived and directed the Navigator work in three cities. There he met his missionary wife, June, also ministering in Romania with The Navigators. They have been married since 1984 and have two grown daughters, Stephanie and Karen.

During his years on staff with The Navigators, Mr. Berger has served as one of five U.S. Directors for the Community ministry, overseeing the development of 175 staff in 125 major cities. He is a conference speaker and continues mentoring other Christian leaders in discipleship, evangelism, ministry funding, and spiritual warfare.

www.EveryManAWarrior.com

Every Man a Warrior is a ministry of The Navigators.